ESCAPE FROM HELL

The Sandakan Story

ESCAPE FROM HELL

The Sandakan Story

by

WALTER WALLACE

London
ROBERT HALE LIMITED
63 Old Brompton Road S.W.7

PRINTED IN GREAT BRITAIN BY
BRISTOL TYPESETTING CO. LTD.
STOKES CROFT - BRISTOL

DEDICATION

To the glorious and everlasting
Memory of those gallant lads
whose lives were sacrificed in
Sandakan, British North Borneo

CONTENTS

by

LIEUT.-GENERAL H. GORDON BENNETT

PREV. COMDG. A.I.F., MALAYA

A N Y W A R story that deals with fighting, imprisonment and escape, from the purely personal side is thrilling and interesting. Especially so is the story of the captivity of prisoners in the hands of the Japanese who raised obstacles and difficulties to the usual Red Cross *mediation*, who refused to furnish detailed lists of prisoners and who would not allow the distribution of Red Cross parcels to our men.

The outside world wonders why there should have been this restriction and seeks to peer through the veil to discover how our men were treated.

There is ample evidence of unnecessary cruelty and harshness by the Japanese captors. They appear to follow the example of their military masters, the Germans. Their natural uncivilised brutality makes them apt pupils—who have been able to teach their teachers many lessons in barbarity.

Fortunately some Japanese officers absorbed Christian principles and treated our men almost normally. Lucky were they that found themselves in prison camps under such commandants.

All civilised people shudder when they hear of German or Japanese harsh treatment, especially in the occupied countries. The effect on the United Nations is to stiffen their determination to fight this war to a finish so that no vestige of power will remain in the Axis Nations, whose wings must be clipped, and whose sinews of war must be severed.

Walter Wallace's book *Escape from Hell,* lifts the veil, and for the first time tells what happened after the official capitulation of Singapore. The story of his escape is full of thrill and interest and has to be read to be enjoyed.

INTRODUCTION

IN PRESENTING my true story, *Escape from Hell: The Sandakan Story*, it may perhaps be of interest to the reader to know a few details of my earlier life. I was born in Sydney, and was educated at Lidcombe and Homebush Public Schools. Being keen on army life, I joined the permanent forces of the Royal Australian Artillery, at Georges Heights, New South Wales, where after an extensive course of study I graduated and became a Sergeant Instructor. Later I was made Senior Recruit Instructor. The twelve years' hard training and the knowledge I thereby gained, fitted me for the work I was afterwards to do when, as an escaped prisoner of war of the Australian Eighth Division, I became also a member of the 125th Infantry Regiment, United States Forces in the Philippines (Guerilla). I am proud of the fact that I was in the unusual position of serving in two armies at the same time.

The fall of Singapore and all that happened then is well-known, so I begin my story with the arrival of " B " Force as prisoners of war at Sandakan, British North Borneo. Early in 1942, the Japanese in Singapore asked for a party of men from the Changi Prison Camp to volunteer to go to an undisclosed destination to perform paid work. This force was known as " A " Force. Soon after the departure of this first party, a second body was called for. This body was to be known as " B " Force, and would comprise fifteen hundred men of all ranks. It was announced that men who were slightly sick would be accepted for this party, as the work to be done was considered light. I was more or less on the slightly sick list, as I had not long been out of the Australian General Hospital, where I had had an operation for acute appendicitis, and I joined this force.

We were bundled into trucks and taken through bomb-damaged Singapore to the wharf, where we were put on board a three-hundred-ton cargo vessel, named *Ubie Maru*. There were two holds forward and one aft, and into these the fifteen hundred of us were packed like sardines. The heat, and the sweat from cramped, ailing bodies made the atmosphere unbearable. There were only three small toilets, hung out over the side of the boat, and to reach them it was necessary to climb a steel ladder. Two meals a day were served during the voyage; they consisted of a yellowish-coloured lime rice, soggy and tasteless. To add to our misery we were kept all the while below decks in fierce tropical heat. After nine days and nights of this veritable hell at sea, we arrived at Sandakan.

It is at this point that I begin my story.

CHAPTER I

THE PRISON SHIP MAKES LAND

I T W A S on the 17th of July, 1942, that our prison ship, *Ubie Maru*, arrived at Sandakan, a village on the north-east coast of British Borneo. The terrific heat of the fierce tropical sun was mellowed that day by a gentle sea breeze which, after the journey from Changi in the fetid hold, crowded to capacity, was refreshing indeed to the fifteen hundred Australian prisoners who were landed on the green slope that came down almost to the water's edge.

Our hearts were filled with relief as we breathed the fresh air, and stretched our limbs, cramped from the terrible crushing in that hell ship's hold. Whatever might lie before us we could, at least, see the sky and move about again. One by one, we moved down the gangway plank, and were counted and re-counted under the direction of our Japanese Commander, Lieutenant Hosijimah, a well-built six-footer with an arrogant personality. Then, heavily guarded, we were marched on to a large green, bordered by a few dwellings and shops, and a picture house. The local inhabitants had been told of our arrival, and had come in their hundreds to see us. Some of them showed signs of pleasure at seeing white men under the domination of the Japanese, but others appeared concerned and distressed.

They had been told not to speak to us, and we had been warned by our guards that no conversation with them would be allowed. But some of us edged our way to where a road bordered the green, and exchanged a few words in mixed English and Malay with some of the bolder spirits. We learnt that we were supposed to have been captured in Australia, which, so the natives had been told, was already in the hands of the Japanese. Contact with the outside world had been completely cut off for the people of North Borneo, for every radio set in the country had been confiscated, and our ship was the first to arrive in the port for months. The inhabitants were dependent upon the Japanese for their news of the war, and that, as we soon gathered, was biased to say the least. It did not, however, take us long to convince some of our listeners that we had been captured in Singapore, and that Australia was still intact.

We sat about on the grass in groups, smoking and talking, wondering what would happen next, and thinking of our loved ones at home. Presently the evening meal arrived. This was of rice, just the same as we had had on the ship, served from dirty, battered buckets. The ration was one cupful per man, eaten without sugar or salt, and washed down with a cup of weak tea without any milk, and also sugarless. As soon as the Japanese thought we had finished, we were mustered and marched off in parties of forty-four, each party escorted by guards in front and at sides and rear. We looked a sight as we toiled along, for we were all of us dirty, untidy and unshaven, there having been no washing facilities at all on board ship.

Leaving the village behind, we climbed a long, winding roadway which seemed as if it would never end. At many points natives stood to watch us pass, and some of them shed tears as they saw the sick and crippled men being pushed along. Eight of us, who were hobbling on sticks, were in the rear and were fortunate in being allowed to rest from time to time. We were in charge of a fat little Japanese soldier, and as we stumbled along we wondered if he could understand English. Since a few unwise words might bring disastrous results, we kept complete silence for a while.

At last the guard grew tired of the silence and tried to converse with us in broken English. It was a feeble attempt, and I asked him if he spoke Malay. It was obvious that he did not, and that left us free to speak to each other in that language, of which we had all picked up a smattering. We felt this to be a small victory over our enemy, and a little later we achieved a better one still. Nearing a cottage, I asked with the help of signs if I might get a drink of water. The guard graciously granted my request, and saluting like a good soldier, I moved off to the cottage. When, a few minutes later, I emerged from having that drink, I had in my possession maps of Borneo and Sandakan, and much valuable information about the countryside.

At last we reached the crest of the hill up which we had been toiling, and entered the grounds of a convent, where we were to rest for the night. It was dark by this time and the only lights in the building were small hurricane lamps, placed here and there, which threw long shadows on the many pillars and the cold stone walls. Bombardier McGlinn and I squatted down in a corner and talked of all the happenings since we had been taken prisoner. I showed him the maps and told him of the information I had been able to obtain during my brief visit to the cottage. I had learned that this region was extremely hot during the day, but that the nights were cool and the air fresh; that in the country round there was dense jungle, interspersed with mangrove swamps infested with reptiles and dangerous animals; that dysentery was rampant in the district, so that we should need to take every precaution possible in our circumstances if we were to preserve our health.

There was little sleep for any of us that night—we were all too tired for sleep. At four o'clock in the morning the Japs aroused us, and counted and re-counted us several times. When they were satisfied that we were all there, we were marched back to the village green for breakfast. The meal consisted of left-overs from the previous evening, reheated. It seemed even more unappetising than before, but not knowing when we should get fed again, we forced ourselves to eat it. As soon as we had eaten, we were mustered again for a march. A doctor examined us to see if any of us were unfit to walk, and fortunately for me I was included in the list of those not considered well enough for the long tramp, as was also McGlinn. A truck arrived to take us, and twenty of us were packed into it, together with two guards. The main body of men had already set out, carrying their light packs, and the driver of our truck set out at a reckless pace to overtake them, racing along the jungle road, and taking corners at a pace that made us cling tightly to anything that was available to avoid being thrown out.

For the most part the road ran in a cutting, with ferns on the sloping banks and palms and rubber trees forming green arches overhead, but here and there we got glimpses of the mountainous, jungle terrain which stretched on either side. Much of this territory had never been explored by white men, and even the natives did not often venture into it for it held death and terrors in many forms. As we racketed along, the sun was rising higher and higher, and soon we were uncomfortably warm, while the glaring light hurt our eyes. It was bad enough for us in the truck, but for those who were marching along that dusty roadway in the tropical sun, it was a thousand times worse. By the time we caught up with them, it was obvious that they were all exhausted. The guards, too, were adding to their sufferings by the treatment they were meting out to them, jabbing with rifle butts at any who were straggling, or kicking them and hitting them with sticks. Our driver edged his way past the marching columns, and soon after that we reached the collection of buildings—a police station, a small power station, a guardroom, and various other buildings—which was to be our prison camp. Here we were unloaded, and left more or less to ourselves to await the arrival of our pals. I lighted a cigarette, and then set myself to study the general layout, to see if there were any way of escaping.

It looked pretty hopeless. The area was small, not more than four or five acres, and was completely surrounded by two barbed wire fences. The inner of these was of the " Double Apron " type. This consists of a line of posts, about eight feet high, with strands of wire, a foot apart, nailed from post to post horizontally, intersected by other strands going from top to bottom, and yet others sloping at an angle of forty-five degrees on each side of the central screen, also interwoven at foot intervals by other strands of barbed wire. Outside this formidable entanglement was another fence, also of barbed wire, of the " Single Apron " type. It meant that, to all intents and purposes, we should be surrounded by five barbed wire fences.

Outside the gate of this enclosure was the main guard-room, and set around at evenly-spaced intervals were seven sentry boxes. Powerful electric lights were installed to illumin-ate the fence at night, to assist the armed guards to make sure that no prisoners escaped under cover of darkness. Escape, indeed, looked to me out of the question on that first day.

However, I continued my survey of the camp. A central road cut straight across it, from the main gate to the back fence, and wooden huts, and native attap-built huts were set on either side of it. Huts for officers' quarters and for kitchens and store-rooms ran along the fence on the gate side. On the left side of the camp, towards the back fence, there was a large pond with a few fish in it, which we soon learnt not to touch on any account, as they ate the mosquitoes. On the right side, close to the gate, stood the biggest and tallest tree I had ever seen. I must have been over two hundred feet high, a wonderful guide for aircraft should any ever decide to pay the camp a visit. Outside the camp, on the north, a large area of ground about a mile in length and perhaps half a mile wide had been cleared of all timber and undergrowth. On the west side, there was a narrow clearing, then jungle. On the south was the road by which we had come, and on the east I could see nothing but thick jungle.

About noon the men struggled into camp. They were in a very bad way, many of them on the verge of collapse. There was to be no mid-day meal, and to make matters worse, a sudden tropical storm broke over us without any warning. In a few moments we were drenched to the skin—and there we were, all fifteen hundred of us, a tired, wet, sick, hungry, downhearted, bunch of Aussies.

Our senior officers lost no time in trying to improve matters. They consulted the Powers-To-Be, inspected the huts and made the necessary allocations. The hut to which I was allocated was the first in the second row to the left of the gate. It was native-built, about twenty feet by ten feet, and was divided into three small rooms. A three foot veranda

B

ran along one side. The hut was raised up from the ground, and access was by means of a few steps. Seventy-five men had to crowd into each hut. When we were all in, we were packed together as tightly as we had been on the prison ship, with no room to sit, let alone lie down.

During the afternoon the kit bags arrived. Most of them were soaked by rain, and some of them had been opened, but we were too wet and hungry and miserable to care about such details. We tried our best to organise ourselves and settle down in our new environment, but it was a hopeless job, and some of us seized our gear and made for the space underneath the hut. The ground was slippery with mud and several of us sat down with more haste than dignity, and we made the discovery that, in spite of our wretched condition, we could still manage to laugh.

At last our evening meal arrived. It consisted again of rice, one cupful of it, with half a cup of some kind of stewed greens and one cup of purple-coloured tea. Several tragedies occurred when men about to sit down to eat slipped in the mud and lost their valuable, though unpalatable, meal. However, those who lost their rations were given another small portion, just enough to stave off absolute starvation.

When the meal was over we returned to our huts, still very hungry, to curse and talk and maybe get some sleep. But sleep was difficult, for the rooms were suffocating, and we were packed so close together that sweat dripped from one body to another, and we became one wet, sticky mass of suffering humanity. There was one low-powered light to each hut, and a few of us tried to read, but it was next to impossible, and it was switched off at nine o'clock anyway. For the most part we talked, mainly about our homes. We had already learnt to be careful of what we said, and it was as well that we had, for in the morning we found that some of the Japs who understood English had crept under the huts to listen to the various conversations.

One of the spies was a suave little man whom we nicknamed the Count. He spoke excellent English, and often mingled with us to try to pick up information. He was well-educated, and during his conversations with us he would often launch into homesick descriptions of the beauty of Japan in Cherry-blossom time. He made a great show of friendliness, and though in our hearts we scorned his overtures, we had to listen to him and pretend to be interested. But I do not think that either he or his fellow-spies ever picked up anything of value from us.

The first and most important thing to see to was camp hygiene. This was supervised by two of our medical stalwarts, Colonel Shepherd and Major Rayson, who, after much argument with the Japanese, succeeded in getting some very necessary improvements carried out. Great credit is due to these two officers for their courage in facing up to the Japs in the matter of sanitation. Had it not been for their efforts, the dysentery which was soon to attack our camp would have taken an even heavier toll of us than it did.

Our first few days in the camp we did practically nothing except answer roll calls and carry out some fatigues and kitchen duties. Most of the time was spent in reading, sleeping, and playing cards. During this time of leisure, many men found their way out of the camp at night, most of them returning before dawn for their expeditions had been made chiefly in the hope of finding some kind of food. We were all suffering from hunger. But a few did not come back, and all that the rest of us could do was to wish them good luck and god-speed in their desperate adventure in which we felt there was but little chance of success. Most of us realised that it was hopeless to attempt to escape at this early stage. It would be necessary to have some knowledge of the country and the people and the dangers of the jungle, as well as some supply of provisions, if there were to be any successful break-out from prison.

From the very beginning of our imprisonment, I had made up my mind to escape if it were humanly possible. My first plans were made with a civilian, Captain Sligo, who had been smuggled in with us as an A.I.F. Officer, though really he was captain of a river boat operating on Malayan rivers. He was about forty years of age, short and slim with a Malayan complexion. He spoke the Malayan language fluently and could pass as a Malay with ease. He and I became good friends, and soon he took me into his confidence and told me of the plans he was making to escape. He had been creeping out of camp at night to collect information, and his arrangements were well in hand. Food, arms, and ammunition, would be available, and even boats would be supplied. There were, he told me, to be two parties. One party, under his control, was to make for the Phillippines, while the other, under my leadership, was to try to reach the Celebes. But the plot never came to maturity, for Captain Sligo went down with dysentery when it came to the camp and died in a couple of days.

Time was beginning to hang heavily on our hands, when suddenly the Japanese Commander, Hosijimah, called a general parade. Speaking to us through an interpreter, although he could speak English well when he chose, he informed us that we were to build an aerodrome for the use of the Imperial Japanese Air Force, with the roads and bridges and anything else that might be necessary to render it serviceable. The work was estimated to take us three years to complete, and we were to be paid at the rate of ten cents a day in Japanese Invasion currency, worth about a hundred cents to the dollar. As the Malayan wage for a coolie averaged two and a half dollars a day, it will be seen that we were not to be overpaid. Frank Martin, who was standing next to me, swore quietly under his breath as he listened.

" Fifteen hundred sick men have been brought to this place to do light work," he said, " and it turns out to be building an aerodrome !"

" Three years, he says it will take," I said. " I bet I'll be out of this place in less than one year. You wait and see."

As soon as the parade was over, parties of men were organised. Some were required for work about the camp, for chopping and carrying in wood for the kitchens and the power station, for gardening, attending to sanitation, and—most unpleasant task of all—for making coffins out of scrap material for the burial of our dead. After these jobs had been allotted, about six hundred men of those left were considered fit enough to undertake the aerodrome construction. The majority of us were not averse to doing it, even if we were not wildly enthusiastic about it. It would be something to do, a release from camp boredom. It meant going outside and seeing something new—about all it meant money, no matter how little, and money meant smokes and momentary contentment.

CHAPTER II

BUILDING THE AERODROME

THE SITE selected for the aerodrome was about three miles to the east of the prison camp. The track that led to it was very rough. We had to climb over fallen trees left by those who had cut the first road to it, and wade through patches of muddy water, taking care not to slip in the slime. If any of us did, we were helped up again by jabs from Japanese bayonets.

That first day we were pleased to be out of the compound. Everything about us was fresh and green and beautiful, and though we were not allowed to touch them, coconut and paw-paw trees towered above us on both sides of the way. But our pleasure was short-lived. When we reached the large clearing where the aerodrome was to be made, we found one of the greatest bullies of all time awaiting us in the person of Lieutenant Okahara of the Imperial Japanese Army. He addressed us and told us in no uncertain manner what we were expected to do. The aerodrome was to be completed in record time, for it was wanted urgently, and we were to work from daylight until dark, digging, shovelling, wheeling barrows of rocks and dirt, and levelling the ground. We gasped as we listened to the words " From daylight to dark." In this climate, under this sun, and we were all half sick men, scheduled for light work!

The guards took over and hustled us to the store to collect picks, shovels, and axes. Then, to shouts of " Speedo! Speedo!" work began. Some of us picked at the rocky ground, others shovelled the dirt we loosed into trucks which were pushed along rails to a dump some eight hundred yards away and then brought back empty for more. Only one short break was allowed between the commencement of work and lunch time, a break just long enough to smoke one cigarette and drink a mug of water, which, for convenience, was kept in buckets close to the work, one bucket to each gang. No one was allowed to drink except at these organised breaks. If anyone tried during working time to quench his overwhelming thirst, the bucket would be kicked over and the man knocked to the ground, or hit with a stick. Our bodies were soon aching agonisingly from the heavy work of digging and shovelling, while the sweat poured from us under the burning sun.

Lunch was served at noon, the food being, as usual, a cup of rice, half a cup of weed stew, and a mug of sugarless, milkless, tea. We were not allowed to look for cover, but had to sit and eat our meal scorched by the sun, while the flies buzzed about us maddeningly. The afternoon work was the same as the morning, except that during our brief break, no smoking was allowed. We grew more and more exhausted as the hours wore on, and sunset was a welcome sight to us all, for at last we could stop work and return to camp.

The Japs must have wanted that aerodrome badly from the way they made us toil at it. Should the required number of workers not be available owing to sickness, a round-up would be made by the guards, and doctors, medical orderlies, and even padres, would be pushed into the working parties. Sometimes they would invade the hospital, and if a patient was so much as able to stand up without help, he would be forced to go out and work. Officers were treated just the same as the rest of us, except that they were paid a little higher. They worked the same hours, in the same way, and ate the same food. The little yellow men refused to recognise their rank, and only the star or the pip which they wore on their shirt lapels showed that they were officers.

After a few days, discipline suddenly tightened up and became very strict. It seemed that we were working too slowly, and Lieutenant Okahara devised a plan to speed us up. He armed a team of our guards with bayonets and pick handles to march up and down our lines and deal out blows to any unfortunate man who paused for a moment to stretch his tired body after bending for hours over a pickaxe or a spade. Some of them threw stones to hurry us along, and it was quite a usual sight to see men knocked down and kicked in the stomach and testicles. I have many ulcers on my legs, due to being kicked violently on the shin by these brutal creatures. Often, too, a whole gang of men would be lined up and made to stand without hats in the blazing sun with arms stretched horizontally sideways, while two Japs would march along the row, one behind and one in front of us, giving each man a crack with a stick on head, back, stomach, or chest, as he passed. It was torture, wicked, ghastly, cruel.

I remember one man, Gunner Desmond Rooke, who, although sick, volunteered to take the place of someone worse than himself. He was not fit to work, and failed to come up to the standard required, so he was made to stand with his arms stretched out in this way, facing the sun, hatless and bootless, for a whole half hour. We were all terribly upset at seeing a good lad treated in this inhuman way, but there was nothing that we could do about it, and, as time went on, we became used to witnessing such sickening sights. The Japanese are at that stage of development where the infliction of physical pain is the only accepted means of correction. But to use such means of punishment on their own men in their own army is one thing—it is a different matter to inflict cruel torture on helpless prisoners of war, and sick men at that.

It was little wonder that our men, under-nourished and over-worked, were often seen shaking with terror on the early morning parade, knowing what would probably happen to them before they returned to camp that night—if they returned at all.

Yet, in spite of the torment and humiliation and exhaustion we endured each day, our captors could not quite break our spirit. As we struggled along the rough track on our homeward way, worn-out though we were, we still managed to sing. It needed only one or two men to start some old song, " Nursie," or " Kiss me Good-night, Sergeant-Major," and suddenly hundreds of other voices would join them, echoing through the jungle. The Commander of the camp, Hosijimah, was staggered at the way we marched back singing, and once asked Major Fleming how it was that Australians could still sing after a long day's work in " Such trying conditions," as he put it. Major Fleming told him that it was because that was the way Australians were made.

In the camp, as well as out at work, the cruelties went on. One afternoon, because of a language misunderstanding, Corporal Ray Coaker was called to the parade ground and made to kneel down on some small broken stones, and, while in this position, was brutally kicked in the face and stomach. The Japanese seemed to delight in thinking out new forms of cruelty of this sort, and we could do nothing about them. There was nobody to whom we could complain, all we could do was to bear our lot as stoically as we could. Occasionally, though, somebody did put up a show of resistance. One lad, who worked in the kitchen rigged up on the aerodrome site, had just brought a bucket of water to use for cooking purposes when a Jap came up and washed his hands in it. Jimmy rebuked him, which so incensed the Japanese soldier that he started to beat up the daring prisoner. Jimmy, however, had been a boxer in civilian life and he rashly retaliated. With a beautiful, well-aimed, smash on the jaw, accompanied by a devastating uppercut, he sent the little yellow man flying, putting him down for the count. It was a wonderful thing to see, but the air seemed to stand still and we all held our breath as we waited for what would happen next.

We did not have long to wait. Half a dozen Japs came surging round and attacked the hero with their pick handles, mercifully soon knocking him into unconsciousness. When he recovered a little, it appeared as though his right arm was broken, and some of our medical orderlies who were working that day on the drome put it into a sling. But the Japanese ripped the sling off and tied Jimmy's arms behind his back. They then made him kneel on a jagged piece of wood and put another jagged piece between the backs of his knees, and then forced him backwards so that he was looking up directly at the sun. For over an hour they kept him in this painful position, throwing cold water over him each time that he collapsed, so that he might receive further torture.

The rest of us were kept well away from him so that there was no possibility of helping him. But even if we had been near him, there was nothing that we could have done. We could only watch miserably, and be thankful when at last the guards took him away back to camp. But his punishment was not yet over. Back in camp they put him in " The Cage ", a devilish contrivance which they had erected for rebels. It was made of battens, and was about four feet square, standing on legs so that it was raised some four feet from the ground. The battens were placed an inch apart from each other, and in the openings were inserted strands of barbed wire. The victim shut up in this cage was allowed no bedding, no evening meal and no breakfast. He had to spend the night in this ghastly prison, and in the morning was taken out and sent off fasting to work again. To keep him just alive he was given a mid-day meal, and when the working day was over he was incarcerated again. This torture went on until the term awarded to him for punishment was over.

It seemed hardly possible that anyone could suffer this punishment for long and live. But Jimmy survived it, and was then sent to another prison camp on the north-west coast of Borneo. From his condition when he was taken away, we had little hope of ever seeing him again, but I heard later that he lived to be liberated and did, eventually, reach home.

Our Force Commander, Lieutenant-Colonel Walsh, made many complaints to Hosijimah about the cruelties inflicted on the men, and about the insufficient food supply and the lack of urgently needed medical necessities. But his complaints did little or no good. Once, it is true, Hosijimah lined us all up on parade, and he and our Colonel and the doctors inspected each man minutely. We were a terrible sight. Our bodies were burned and blistered from the scorching sun, and already emaciated from want of proper nourishment, and our legs were scarred from wounds inflicted by the Japs, many of which had ulcered. But though we hoped that better conditions might come after this close inspection, nothing happened. Hosijimah made us a speech reminding us that we had volunteered for the work, and saying that he was not responsible for anything except to see that we did it. And then we were sent off back to the aerodrome site.

Deaths were increasing in number now daily, and soon dysentery entered the camp to augment the toll. This did seem to worry our gaolers a little, and a high rank Japanese medical officer visited us to confer with our own doctors. But all he could suggest was an old-fashioned remedy of mixed charcoal and sulphur, and as we had none of either, his visit did nothing to help us. All that we could do was to kill every blowfly that we could, in an attempt to stop the sickness from spreading, and be as careful as possible with our spoons and dishes.

The Isolation Hut was a ghastly place to visit. I went there sometimes to see a stricken friend, and it was appalling to see the men lying there, mere shadows of their former selves, with sunken eyes, and excreta pouring from them, defying all the efforts the orderlies made to keep them comfortable. And night by night more sufferers succumbed to the plague, and each day more wooden boxes were carried out to a special cemetery close to the convent where we had spent our first night in Sandakan.

All this suffering and death might have been avoided had Japan kept the promises she had made when she signed the Geneva Convention regarding the treatment of prisoners of war.

While so many of our men were suffering in the camp hospital, those of us considered fit enough to work still had to endure ill-treatment at work. On the aerodrome site blows were still the order of the day. Then suddenly, for a little while, they stopped. The Japs had had what they thought was a brain-wave to speed up their tired slaves. To the ten men who had worked the best were presented little square pieces of wood, which, when handed in at lunch time, entitled the holders to a mug of unsweetened coffee. But after three days of this unexpected liberality, the issue of coffee tickets was stopped. One of our bright boys copied the squares and the lettering on them, and instead of ten of them being presented, two hundred were handed in. Thus ended the coffee ration.

Singing was the only relaxation we had, and we made the most of it. In camp at night was the time when we mostly indulged in it, when we were sitting round the little fires lighted in holes in the ground for the purpose of warming up our left-over portions of rice. Someone would start a tune, his hut companions would pick it up, and in a few minutes the whole camp would be singing *Waltzing Matilda, I've Got Sixpence, She'll Be Coming Round The Mountain When She Comes*. Those songs still bring back the echo of my comrades' voices, and if I shut my eyes I can see again the flickering fires with the tired men sitting round them, and overhead, perhaps, the Southern Cross, our national emblem, shining down upon us, bringing us a message of comfort and hope.

Smoking was permitted only in certain areas, and smokers had to go to one of them before lighting their cigarettes, each taking with him a tin of water into which to drop his ash, for with the native-built attap huts fire was an ever-present danger. In the early stages of our imprisonment, we each received a ration of ten cigarettes a fortnight. Then, owing to shipping difficulties, it was reduced to seven. Later, it was cut to five, and then to none at all. However, we could still purchase small quantities of native tobacco at the canteen, which, although it did not taste much like tobacco, was better than nothing at all. Cigarette paper then become the problem, and, one by one, our limited supply of books began to disappear as pages were abstracted for the purpose of rolling cigarettes. Even Bibles and prayer-books, I am sorry to say, were mutilated in this way by the smoke-starved men.

Matches were another scarcity. But fortunately some of us possessed magnifying glasses, so, in that hot sun, this difficulty could be overcome.

Sunday was supposed to be a day of rest, but although we did not go to work on the aerodrome, our camp guards found plenty for us to do. We were set to clean up the camp, and cut the grass between the two outside fences. However, our padres insisted upon finding time to conduct Church services, and these were always well attended. They often brought great relief as we listened to the comforting and encouraging words especially chosen for our situation.

The Japanese now took to posting up news bulletins on a notice board. These were simply terrific. There were glorious victories everywhere—all for the Japs. The Nippon Air Force shot down hundreds of American and Australian planes, and bombed Allied shipping and ammunition dumps every day, and always " All planes returned safely." Their navy, too, accomplished marvels. They sank ships of all classes by the score without ever losing a vessel themselves, while their soldiers captured everything it was possible to capture without ever losing a life in doing it. To crown it all, there would often be a piece tagged on describing how the people of the captured territory, rejoicing at being freed from captivity, were " co-operating " with the Nippon Army which had " relieved " them. We could guess how " relieved " they were and how well they would be " co-operating !"

One day a notice appeared on the board saying. " To help the Australian Prisoners of War to keep up their good spirits," the Commanding Officer would grant them " a day's sport." Lists of events were posted up, together with details of the prizes to be won. These were to be fowls, bananas, and paw-paws,—which, incidentally, the Japs pinched from the local farmers. All prisoners, except those actually in bed in hospital, were allowed to attend the sports, which were held on the aerodrome site. Race after race was run, hurdles were jumped, and the whole thing was an outstanding success at the time. But there proved to be a catch to this " good deed " business. The Japs now knew exactly how fit we really were. If those on the sick list were able to walk out to the aerodrome and back without actually collapsing—why, then, they were fit enough to do light duty. And so, as a result of our Sports Day, the working parties gained an immediate increase.

During the lunch break on the aerodrome site, the local inhabitants were allowed to sell us small portions of fish and fruit, from an area barricaded off for the purpose. Among the sellers who dealt in a kind of fritter, there was a young middle-aged Chinese. His name, Heng Joo Meng, is one that will long be remembered by many of us. He lived with some friends in the jungle, not far from the aerodrome, and spoke excellent English. He seemed so intelligent and alert that I wondered what on earth a man of his calibre was doing selling fritters. One day, as I was looking at him, I caught his eye and winked at him. He winked back, and I edged my way towards the barricade until I was close enough to say " Hello ! How are you getting on ?"

He answered in a rather subdued manner : " No very good. We very hungry. Have you rice, please?"

The next day, Frank Martin and I took some of our breakfast rice out with us, and at lunch time we exchanged it with Heng Joo Meng for a couple of pieces of fish. In this manner began a friendship which was going to mean a very great deal to me. After a few more days of this bartering, I arranged with Heng Joo Meng to slip away and meet me in the jungle, pretending to the guards that I needed to relieve my bowels. The ruse succeeded, and I was able to snatch a few minutes conversation with Heng Joo Meng. He told me that he wanted to be my friend, and he expressed great happiness when I told him that I was his friend for life. He had lived in Singapore with his wife and two children, and when the Japs invaded the island, he had moved to Sandakan, hoping that he might be of use to the Allied cause as a guerilla. He needed rice badly, and as we hated the stuff, Frank and I made some very good swaps. From time to time we would hide in a prearranged spot all the rice that we could spare, while, in exchange, he would plant for us fruit, fish, and turtle-eggs.

We needed a radio set urgently in camp, for we wanted to get correct news, to offset the poppycock the Japs dished out to us, and to buck up the morale of the men, especially of those in hospital. So one day, as Heng Joo Meng and I sat chatting under a palm tree I asked him if he could possibly produce a radio. He said that all the radio sets on the island had been taken by the Japanese, but that he would do his best to find one for me. I promised that if I was caught with it in my possession, I would say that I had found the parts in the jungle, so that no one would ever know that it had come from him.

A few days later, I was again sitting under the palm tree

which was our meeting place, when my friend slipped round from behind a trunk, with a big smile on his face and a still bigger parcel in his arms. It contained the parts of a radio set, and I jumped for joy as I asked him how he had got it. He told me that along the road was a locked-up shed in which were several dismantled sets. He had got in through a window and brought these parts along.

The parcel was far too big to carry back to camp as it was, so I had to take a few pieces in at a time. Some of the parts I I tied between my legs, under my legs, under my trousers, screws and other small bits I hid in my boots and in my hat. It took several days to get everything back, and Major Fleming was very worried when he knew what I was doing, and warned me to be most careful. I was certainly running a great risk, but I brought all the parts safely in eventually, and the set was then soon assembled by some of the signallers. Now we were able to get the real news, which proved to be very different from the bull-shit we had been receiving, and it was wonderful how much happier and more contented we all were in consequence. So was Heng Joo Meng when I passed it on to him at our jungle meetings.

Joo Meng—he told me that this was his "given" name, Heng being his surname—belonged to the Sandakan Underground Movement. There were several police officers in this, as well as a civilian medical man, Dr. J. P. Taylor. This doctor was an Australian, but he had been allowed to continue his practice under Japanese control. The Sandakan Underground was a link in a chain of similar organisations scattered throughout the territories occupied by the Japanese. They had already done much good work, carrying out acts of sabotage and giving assistance to prisoners of war. Joo Meng himself handled large quantities of medical supplies provided by Dr. Taylor. Under cover of darkness these would be planted in and around the prisoner-of-war cemeteries, to be picked up by bearers at funerals and smuggled into the camps.

With Joo Meng's assistance, I now began seriously to plan an escape. He obtained maps and charts for me, and drew a map of Sandakan, plotting every guard post with the number of Japs in each, and marking on it each wharf, signal and

wireless station, and storage dump in the district. Also he gave
me instruction in jungle lore teaching me how to recognise the
various trails, how to find water, and what to eat and not to
eat. He promised me, too, that when I needed it, a boat and
food would be forthcoming for my use. One of the most
useful lessons he taught me was how to move quietly in the
jungle.

" This way," he said. " Look ! Heel and toe, gently, firmly,
slowly," and, after a little practice I found that I had grasped
the idea. After that, I practised the movement as often as I
could, knowing how essential silence would be when I made
my escape.

One day Joo Meng gave me a surprise. There was a
Guerilla Unit, he told me, on the island of Tawi Tawi, about
two hundred miles east of us, one of the Philippine group. The
officer commanding the Unit was an American-Philippino
named Suarez. This news put new life into me, for two hundred
miles of sea in a trustworthy boat would not be an impossible
journey, and it would be a goal for which to make. However,
I have always been a believer in the old adage " More haste,
less speed," and I was determined to go slowly and lay my
plans very carefully.

The first thing to be done, we thought, was to write to the
Commanding Officer at Tawi Tawi, so Frank and I sat down
to compose a letter. We told him where we were and how we
were being treated, and how great was our need for help. I
gave this letter to Joo Meng, who passed it on to one of his
friends for transit. Frank and I then told Major Fleming
what we had done. He was terribly worried and said that we
had taken a tremendous risk, but it was too late for him to do
anything about it. All he could do was to make us promise
to let him know when, if ever, our messenger returned.

Day after day we waited in trepidation, our suspense growing with every hour that passed. I felt quite ill with anxiety
at times, wondering what would happen if the Japs caught
the runner and found the letter. It had my name on it. Judg-
ing by the treatment meted out for trivial offences, my end
would be a pretty grim one if the letter fell into enemy hands.
I don't quite know how I endured that time of waiting, but

after about three weeks, Joo Meng greeted me one day with the words : " All is well."

I breathed again. It was as though some terrific load had been lifted from my shoulders. Looking back now, I don't quite know what I expected from my exploit. A handful of men in an enemy-occupied island two hundred miles away could not, with the best will in the world, do much to help us in our plight. But at the time I felt greatly encouraged to know that someone, allied with us in the same cause and not too far distant, knew of our existence and would, if opportunity occurred, try to help us. I told Major Fleming that all was well, and he went white with relief and gave Frank and me a lecture to the effect that we must never do such a thing again. But he had another shock coming to him—I informed him that I was going to try to escape.

He looked at me with eyes that nearly popped out of his head.

" Well, of course, I can't stop you from trying, Wallace," he said. " But I do beg of you to reconsider what you propose doing. I assure you that you have no chance whatever of getting away from this place."

He was genuinely concerned about us, and his arguments, I think, did do something to deter Frank, who, in the end, decided not to join in the attempt. But they only made me all the more determined to do my utmost to escape from this hell. It would be difficult, but I thought that with careful planning it could be done. I would take my time, and go about the matter slowly and methodically, leaving nothing within my power undone to ensure success.

C

CHAPTER III

THE OPENING OF THE AERODROME

THERE HAD been many more deaths in the camp, and several men had escaped. The Japs were worried, not about the deaths, but about the escapes, and a general parade was called at which we were addressed by a Major Suga who, after telling us how fortunate we were to be living in such a good camp in such wonderful conditions, warned us against trying to get away from it. It would be very foolish of us to attempt to do so, he told us, for we would almost certainly be caught and severely dealt with. Even if the Japanese did not get us, the wild animals that lived in the jungle most certainly would.

A few days later we awoke in the morning to find that the camp was surrounded by soldiers, and that machine guns and mortars were trained upon us. We wondered fearfully what was going to happen now, but after a while we found that all this show of force was for the purpose of a special kit inspection. Each man had to stand beside his bed and lay out his few possessions to be examined by the Japanese soldiers. Nothing of any importance was discovered, as anyone who owned a knife or a camera always took care to keep it carefully concealed. I had a camera which Joo Meng had got for me, and one of the engineers had removed the bottom from my water bottle so that the camera could be carried inside without anyone dreaming it was there. I carried it about the aerodrome with me and took several snapshots as evidence of the cruelties practised upon us by the guards, but unfortunately camera and films were lost during the escape.

When we had laid out our possessions, we were herded back to the parade ground, where we were addressed by our boss, Hosijimah. He read aloud to us a paper, telling us to listen very carefully. The paper said :

> " 1. We abide by the rules and regulations of the Imperial Japanese Army.
> 2. We agree not to attempt to escape.
> 3. Should any of our soldiers escape we request that you shoot him to death."

" All men will now move up to the table and sign this document," announced Hosijimah.

For a few minutes there was a deathly silence. No one moved or spoke. Then Hosijimah turned to Colonel Walsh and ordered him to come up to the table and sign the document. The colonel moved forward to the table and picked up the paper.

" I will re-read this to you," he said to us. Then, loudly and clearly he read again the words we had just heard. When he had done so he threw the paper on the ground and proclaimed vehemently :

" I, for one, will not sign such a paper as this."

You could have heard a pin drop as he made this declaration. We stood waiting breathlessly, wondering what the next move would be. Hosijimah needed no interpreter to tell him what Colonel Walsh had said. Immediately he ordered that he should be arrested, and with his hands tied behind his back he was marched outside the gate, where his captors turned him round to face us. Six soldiers pointed their loaded rifles at him, while others trained the machine guns on to us and stood with hand grenades ready to throw. The tension was almost unbearable. If Colonel Walsh had given the word, I believe that every man of us would have surged forward to his assistance, no matter how many of us lost our lives.

But he did not give the word. He stood in complete silence, never flickering an eyelid, and without some cue from him we did not know what to do. Then Major Workman, always a quick thinker, came to the rescue. Picking up the paper, he moved quickly up to Hosijimah and suggested an alteration to that abominable third clause, to which, perhaps thinking he had gone too far, the Japanese commander agreed. The clause now read :

" I know that if I escape I will be shot," and this new draft was read aloud to us, and then signed by us all under protest.

We still had to remain on parade for some time longer, while yet another examination of the huts took place. When at last we were dismissed, we found that all our pencils and writing materials had been taken away, in an attempt to prevent any of us from communicating with the outside world. A little later, Colonel Walsh was released, and at last the working parties were marched off to the aerodrome.

On our return to camp that evening, we were issued with small pieces of cloth on which were stamped our prison numbers, which had to be fixed to the front of our hats. My number was 612. This new idea was to save time in checking prisoners. It worked well from our point of view as well as from theirs.

Frank still had not made up his mind whether or not he would try to escape with me, but for a while he continued to help me in making my plans. We had now to be even more careful than before, and in order to make our correspondence with Joo Meng safer, we devised a code consisting of human figures, letters, and semaphore signs, changing it every week. This new kind of crossword puzzle gave us some headaches, but we found it very interesting puzzling out Joo Meng's message to us.

Meanwhile, the aerodrome was taking shape. Hills had been carted away, trees cut down, roots dug out, holes filled in. Many workers had died, but floggings continued as usual, and life was one continuous hell. Whenever I could, I changed my jobs, one day working on the drome itself, the next cutting wood, then joining the gangs toiling on the roads. I did this because I wanted to study the lay-out of the surrounding territory as much as possible, to find out what cover and water there was, what food one might find, and anything else that might help in my escape plans. I was a sergeant at the time and so was able to attach myself more or less to what party I liked.

Life was a strange mixture at that time. Ghastly things were happening to us, and none of the small comforts prisoners of war received from more civilised captors ever came our way. No mail was ever received, not even Red Cross parcels, although we heard that many of these were arriving in Singapore. Nor were we allowed to send any letters. During my stay at Sandakan, the only mail home we were allowed to send was one card from each man, stating, " I am well. I am working for wages." There were many grim remarks made as we signed these cards. True enough, we were working for wages —ten cents a day. And to the Japs if a man was alive he was considered to be well, though I doubt if many of our relatives would have thought much of our state of health if they could have seen us. Hungry and tired and emaciated, our nerves shattered to bits, and our bodies scarred and ulcerated by the many beatings we received, we looked more like walking skeletons than living men. Our clothes, too, were in a terrible condition, for there were no replacements. We usually went to work wearing no boots or socks, no shorts or shirts—just in a pair of dirty underpants, or with a piece of towel draped round our loins. Most of us, it is true, did possess a hat of sorts, but a hat after it has been soaked with rain and sweat, scorched in the sun, used to drink out of and bath in, and to swat flies with, is not an article of clothing to add much to a man's appearance.

Yet in spite of all our misery and suffering, there were things that made us laugh at times. There was the time when a steam roller was wanted, and the Japs pinched one from Singapore and shipped it over to our island. It was brought up to the aerodrome site, and started chugging up and down the runway while the Japs stood round to admire. Suddenly, it somehow managed to manœuvre itself on to a boggy patch, purposely designed to trap any Allied planes that might try to pay us a visit, and disappeared from the face of the earth. The noise created by the Nips at this catastrophe was truly alarming, and we forgot our woes in the excitement that followed, when with ropes and lorries and everyone lending a

38   ESCAPE FROM HELL

hand, Puffing Billy was slowly hauled out of the mud and brought back to solid ground again.

Then there was the time when we had a talkative little guard with whom we used to make conversation during our rest period, in the hope that he would forget the time and allow us a few minutes longer to sit and smoke. We would listen meekly to a bull-shit talk about Japan, and then turn the conversation to the war situation. This seemed to please him immensely, and he would decribe what was happening— Japanese version—with comical gestures. One day, one of the Aussies asked him how the bombing was going, and clasping his hands rapturously over his head to represent a Nippon bomber, he showed us how it would dive down over our Australian cities, and then, cringing abjectly, he demonstrated how our people ran for cover in a raid.

" Darwin bombed very good," he told us enthusiastically.

" How about Townsville?" asked somebody.

" Townsville—Bomb! Bomb! Bomb!" said our little Jap.

" And Sydney?" asked somebody else.

"Yes, Sydney bombed, too. Australia nearly captured— Tasmania still fighting," elaborated the little yellow man.

" What about Luna Park?" chirped up someone, looking for a weak point in the babbling story.

Yes, Luna Park had copped it, too. So had Mae West, so had Shirley Temple. The game looked like going on for ever when one silly ass said :

" What about Tokio?"

This question put an end to the fun. The little man sprang to his feet, and after cursing us with every swear word in the Japanese dictionary, sent us back to work in double quick time.

Then there was our camp concert. Once, when Hosijimah was in a good mood, he decided that we might arrange a concert in the camp. It was really amazing what a lot of talent was forthcoming. We found that we had enough singers, elocutionists, musicians, and magicians, to make up a really good show. The engineers built up a rather rickety stage, and Hosijimah actually found for us a piano, two violins, and a set of drums. True, the piano had ten strings missing, and the violins had seen their best days, and only one drum had a skin. But these were difficulties which we were all on our mettle to overcome, and after some evenings of rehearsals we were ready for the gala night. Our chorus girls were the queerest set of glamour beauties that anyone ever clapped eyes on—skinny legs, bow legs, hairy legs, and breasts that slipped off and fell on the floor as their owners danced around. The music was a series of discords, but we did some really excellent sketches, and ill and exhausted as we all were, we found that we could still laugh. I did some card tricks, which came off quite well until I started on one which needed a shirt sleeve to complete it, and I suddenly realised that I had no shirt nor even a trouser pocket into which to slip the disappearing card. The only thing left for me to do was to swallow it. It was the toughest meal I've ever eaten.

The whole affair was a great success, and Hosijimah talked about having a repeat show. But there never was one. Apparently the Japanese lost a few cruisers, Hosijimah's mood changed, and our stage, piano, violins, and drums, disappeared.

It was a good thing we had these few breaks in the misery of our imprisonment, for our general condition was worsening all the while. Our medical supplies had run out, and had it not been for the efforts of Dr. Taylor, who continued to arrange for the most urgently needed drugs to be smuggled into camp, the death-roll would have been even greater than it was. Sickness was daily increasing, many of the lads had become insane, and deaths were numerous. Funerals were carried out always with as much solemnity and dignity as was possible in the circumstances. The coffins could only be of plain packing-case wood, but on each would rest a wreath of vines and wild flowers, together with the hat of the deceased man. Bearers would carry this simple coffin slowly and reverently to a lorry waiting at the main gate. The lorry was, of course, driven by a Japanese driver and carried two Japanese guards, but it would have also several of our own men aboard —the bearers, a padre, and another officer. At the cemetery the service was read by our padre, the coffin was lowered into the grave by our bearers, and our bugler sounded the Last Post.

Today there is no Australian cemetery at Sandakan. The bodies were later removed and re-interred in a special cemetery in Labuan.

As our first year of captivity drew to a close, our work on the aerodrome began to show results, and soon arrangements were being made to receive the first plane from Kuchin. The Japs were very excited, and plans were laid for a big opening day. Several big shots would be attending, and the place was to be dressed up for the occasion. The natives were given the task of decorating, and palm leaves and vine tendrils and masses of jungle flowers were collected. A huge floral archway was erected at the drome entrance, and other arches were placed at strategic points. Japanese flags were waving everywhere, and small hand ones were given out to the local population to carry.

The great day arrived. We were ordered to attend the opening, and were told to be clean and tidy. We did our best, though we had nothing to wear but the underpants and bits of towelling which we wore every day. Still, we washed, and combed our hair, and some of us even had a shave. At the entrance the police decided that we must be searched just in case any of us carried some secret weapon or grenade, though where we could have concealed any such thing it was difficult to see. Still, the search was duly carried out, and when nothing was discovered we were marched on to the site. There we were lined up, looking like nothing on earth, while close by were rows of Malay and Chinese workers dressed up in A.I.F. trousers and shirts—the replacement equipment which ought to have been issued to us.

There were crowds of people there—not that many of them wanted to be, but they were given no choice. They were told they had to turn out, and having had bitter experience of what the Japs might do to them if they didn't, they thought it better to obey. Soon the noise of approaching motor bicycles turned everyone's attention to the roadway, and our chief, Hosijimah, in a large black sedan, sporting a pennant, drove up with his escort. A little later the sound of aircraft caused us all to look up at the sky. Three planes came into sight, two fighters and a bomber. The natives grew quite hysterical in their excitement, shouting and waving their flags as the planes circled the drome. Then the bomber left the escorting fighters and glided down to earth. We Aussies had hoped that it might strike the soft patch which had swallowed the steam roller. But there was no such luck. It made a perfect landing.

We did not know who the big-wig was who stepped out of the bomber, but he must have been somebody important for all the local officials treated him as though he were a god. They saluted and bowed low from the hips and did everything except kiss him. He was in full ceremonial dress, jack boots, gloves, and an enormous sword which nearly tripped him every time he moved, and he was plastered all over with ribbons and badges. He was escorted to a decorated dais and more bowing took place. We had to bow, too, to our immense disgust. One Aussie near me toppled right over as he bowed and fell flat on his face. But he picked himself up as we raised our bodies and our Jap guards did not notice.

The speeches then began in earnest, but none of us knew what they were about, for they were all in Japanese. Even the natives could not have understood them. However, everyone continued to cheer and clap at every opportunity until at last the ceremony was over, and while the great men went off to a marquee to continue the celebrations wtih refreshments, we were marched back to camp.

And so the first section of the Sandakan Aerodrome, built by Australian prisoners of war at the cost of a few invasion dollars, plus hundreds of valuable lives, was opened.

CHAPTER IV

THE ESCAPE FROM CAMP

CHRISTMAS HAD come. It was our first Christmas as prisoners of war—and my last as such. I had not been idle with my plans during the last few months, but I had had to move very cautiously, and be very much on the alert as to what I said and to whom I spoke. Frank, although he had now decided not to come with me, did all he could to help me, and it was good to have him as a confidant during this waiting time.

We all felt depressed and sad on Christmas Eve, thinking of our homes and our loved ones, wondering when, if ever, we should see them again. The stars were beautiful that night, I remember, and we sat on the ground, looking at them, singing Christmas carols from time to time. Then, as the moon rose, we had a little surprise from our officers. Draped in sheets, to represent dwellers in Bethlehem at the time of the Nativity, they came over the mound in the north-east section of the camp, singing in unison, *Holy Night, Silent Night,* and we all stopped our own singing to listen. It was a moving experience, and I think that not many of us were dry-eyed as we listened to those voices. Even the Japanese guards kept still to hear. To this day, the music of that lovely hymn moves me to tears, as it brings back the picture of that night under the stars, making me think of how many of those who heard it then have passed away into the " Silent Night." Passed away, not because they were killed in war, but because of what they suffered at the hands of a cruel, power-drunk enemy.

Our captors had not provided very much extra for us on

Christmas Day. For breakfast we had the usual rice, with a small piece of barely-eatable fish. After breakfast we were sent out to cut the grass between the two outer barbed wire fences. I was glad of this job, because I wanted to examine those fences at close quarters, to see if there were any broken strands of wire or other loophole to offer a chance of escape. There was nothing wrong with the fences anywhere, but I made an important discovery. My skinny, shrunken body was now so thin, that by lying flat on the ground I should be able to crawl underneath the wires nearest to the ground. This was a most important discovery, and it sent my spirits soaring, as it did Frank's later, when I told him of it.

My spirits rose even higher at dinner-time. The Japanese had only provided a watery kind of stew, with a small piece of yak meat, about a spoonful of yak to each man, a cup of rice, and a paw paw to be divided between eight men. But Frank and I and a few of our closest friends had a wonderful treat. Joo Meng had planted a parcel for me in the jungle the day before, with instructions that it was not to be opened until Christmas Day. I untied it that night, feeling like an excited small boy, and we all gaped in amazement as I unwrapped the banana leaves in which the contents were hidden. There were two cooked fowls, fried fish, fried rice, some native cakes, six turtle eggs, fruit, cigarettes and matches, with a note saying: "A Merry Xmas to my good mates, Wal and Frank. H.J.M."

I felt like crying as I looked at these good things. We did not waste much time looking at them, though. We attacked the feast at once and soon made short work of this heavenly gift.

Christmas over, we were set to work upon the building of some new barracks, intended to house some recruits who were on their way to relieve the seasoned troops in charge of our district, who, in their turn, were urgently needed farther south. In due course the recruits arrived. They turned out to be Koreans, and after a few lessons from their Japanese masters, they were soon belting us and throwing stones at us with the best. They were often in trouble themselves, though, and it was a pleasant change for us to see Koreans getting some of the medicine usually reserved for us.

While we were building the barracks, some of us got talking one day to a Japanese N.C.O. who was in charge of us, and we asked him the usual questions about the war.

" All working well for Nippon," he told us, and went on to inform us what was going to happen when Australia was captured, as it soon would be. All patients in mental hospitals and people too old to work would be shot. So would be all the prisoners in Australian gaols.

" If those people cannot be loyal to their own people, it is certain they would not be good for us. So, bang, bang, bang! They all die quick!" said our informant. All young, fertile males were to be castrated. As for the girls : " We breed with all girls," said our Jap.

Plans for my escape were now moving fast. Joo Meng was constantly in touch with me, giving me all the help and advice that he could. I wanted him to come with me, but though he would have liked to do so had he been single, he had a wife and children in Singapore. The Japanese, he knew, would take reprisals against them if he were missed and it were suspected that he had gone with me.

I approached two of our officers, Major Fleming and Lieutenant Goode, asking if they would help me with money and with weapons, if possible. But they refused, telling me that they could not give any assistance to anyone trying to do such a foolhardy thing as I was planning to do, warning me that the odds against success were something like two hundred to one against. I thought about going to some of the other officers, but in the end decided not to do so. I felt that they would probably all stick together in this matter, and it was possible that some of them might take active steps to stop me from making the attempt if I talked too much about it.

So I turned my attention to the ranks, and finally selected two men, Howard Harvey, a strong lad of about twenty-four years of age, and Daniel MacKenzie, also known as Dan MacKay, who was somewhat older. They were both from the Eighth Division Signal Unit, and were both keen to join me when I laid my plan before them.

Although Frank would not join us in escaping, he did all he could to help us in our preparations. One of the things we had to do was to study the movements of the sentries, to see if any of them were careless in the performance of their duties, if they talked with one another after dark, or occasionally slipped away for a few moments. Howard and Mac undertook to watch each night on the north and east fences, while Frank and I watched the south and west. Night after night we watched for several hours, from dusk until it was necessary to go to sleep. It was boring, but our vigil was rewarded at last. One dark night, at about nine o'clock, I noticed that the sentry who had just taken up a position on Number Two post, kept looking in the direction of Post Number Three. After a few moments, he began to walk towards it, at the same time the sentry on Number Three came to meet him. They met halfway, and stood talking together for a little while.

This was important information for us, and I took particular notice of the sentry and the length of time he was away from his post. This same man was on guard duty in the day time, when we were working on the aerodrome, and I told Frank, Mac, and Howard, to watch him carefully, and, if possible, to get into conversation with him. Anything, that we could find out about him, his friends, his habits, his chief interests, might be useful.

The next night we all gathered near the south-west corner, where we could keep an eye upon Number Two post. At nine, the same sentry arrived to take up the same position. He waited there a few moments, then moved as before towards Number Three, remained away for a minute or two, then came back to his own post. We four then strolled along the south fence, behind the store room and the vegetable shed, then we sat down once more, and, keeping up a pretence of casual conversation, we studied the fences and tried to reckon just how long it would take us to clear them. We calculated that it would take about three minutes to get through them all. As we sat there, Howard asked me why we did not try to make our escape when we were out working on the aerodrome, where there would be no fences to negotiate and where, as I had proved by my many meetings with Joo Meng, it was quite possible to slip away into the jungle.

" The reason," I told him, " is simple. You know how they

check up on us from time to time out on the drome. If we tried to get away from there we might get an hour's start, or we might get only five minutes before they called a roll. The moment they found we were gone, the search would begin. And, too, there's the difficulty of getting our gear out to the aerodrome. No! It's better to go from camp in the night. We can take our gear with us, and if we get through the fences successfully, we should have a twelve-hour start before any action would be taken."

" You win," said Howard.

Meanwhile, while we waited for our plans to be complete, an order went out from our captors that we were to learn the Nippon language. Directly after the evening Roll Call, we had to gather close together for instruction. Laurie Maddock was appointed instructor as he knew something of the language. With a Japanese instructor beside him he mounted a platform. The Jap would give him a word, Laurie would repeat it, then tell us its English meaning. Then we all had to call out the Japanese word, time after time, until we had mastered it. Some of our fellows couldn't resist the chance of playing a joke which this proceeding offered. Instead of the Japanese word, they would call out some appalling obscenity, and I encountered some of the worst language I ever heard during " Community Singing," as this phase of our training came to be called.

Joo Meng had given me a geography book about Borneo which I studied assiduously, for I wanted to learn all I could about the jungle and the dangers we should have to meet in it if we succeeded in escaping from the camp. It wasn't reassuring—indeed, the pictures alone were enough to scare the devil himself if he should see them, without any necessity of reading the letterpress. Frank would look a me with a grin when he heard my horrified whistle as I read it, and say :

" What am I going to tell your wife when I get home? I'm sure she'll never forgive me for letting you go on this mad adventure."

But my confidence in the project was unabated, and I would grin back at him and tell him :

" I think the boot will be on the other foot! It will be a

matter of what will *your* wife say to me because I didn't bring you back."

Joo Meng was now a ganger in charge of a company of coolies working on the aerodrome. This would have given us many opportunities to talk together, but we did not take advantage of them, for we feared a trap. Joo Meng had noticed that he had in his gang a man who had been seen collaborating with the Japanese, and he was wary in consequence. So we ignored each other in public, and met only when we could slip into the jungle for a little while, when he handed over to me the various things we should need for our escape which we then smuggled into camp. These included three long jungle knives, called parangs, a revolver, binoculars, a compass and a camera. I also had a small sharp knife made from a stolen Japanese saw which an engineer had fashioned for me. These things were concealed above our beds which were underneath the hut. The three of us had pooled some of our cash and bought some rice and corn, and, in addition, I had two hundred dollars stowed away.

There came a morning when the sentry we had been watching so carefully marched out to the aerodrome in charge of the team with which Frank and I were to work. He was very proud of himself that day, for he had just been made a lance corporal, and on the strength of his promotion he gave me his rifle to carry while he strutted along beside me with his hands in his pockets.

"Me, Lance Corporal," he told me with pride, showing me his badge of office. "Me, Lance Corporal!"

I nodded my admiration and thought to myself: I wonder how long he'll be that! For I had made up my mind, then and there, that tonight was to be The Night. If I missed the chance now, it might never come again, for since our defaulting sentry was now a lance corporal, it was possible that he might soon be promoted to other duties.

During the morning I told Frank, Howard, and Mac, that Zero Hour was to be at nine o'clock that night. Poor Frank looked suddenly ill, but managed to control himself. Howard and Mac became excited and said that it was "About time." At our lunch break, I saw Joo Meng and told him exactly

what we intended to do. He put his arms round me and said:
" Wally, I sincerely wish you all the luck in the world. I
like you a lot and I'm mighty proud of you, and if ever there
is anything more I can do for you, don't hesitate to let me
know. Goodbye for now! See you in Australia later," adding,
as he smiled his goodbye: " Pick up a parcel here later on."

It was a painful moment for me, for I knew that I was saying goodbye to a loyal and devoted friend. Later on that afternoon, under pretext of needing to go to the bush latrine, I
picked up a small parcel and carried it safely back to camp.

Everything went on normally that evening, just as I wanted
it to do. We showed neither hurry nor excitement though I,
for one, was actually on pins and needles within. We had our
tea as usual, and then came Roll Call. Yes, we were all there,
present and correct. After that there was our language lesson,
our " Community Singing." I joined in substituting swear
words for the Japanese ones myself that night, just to be in the
swing of things. When we went to our huts afterwards,
Howard and Mac told their room-mates that they were going
to move out and sleep under the hut. It was so hot and stuffy
inside, they said. There would be more fresh air outside. Nobody seemed to think this at all unusual, and they moved their
gear to my quarters and we all sat talking while we waited for
the moment to arrive.

At eight-forty-five we began moving. One by one, allowing about ten seconds' interval between each move, we slipped
off to the position underneath the vegetable shed, which I
had used as an observation post a few nights back. Here we
waited in silence, a silence in which I could feel my heart
throbbing. As the minutes dragged slowly by my brain was
working overtime, wondering feverishly if our sentry friend
would be on guard that night, if he would still be on Number
Two post, if he would again go as usual for the few minutes'
chat with his companion. Frank was close beside me, Howard
and Mac were near by. All of us had our eye fixed on Number Two post. The night was dark, very dark, not even a star
was to be seen. The only light came from the electric lights
around the fences which threw deep shadows towards the
huts. Conditions were as perfect as we could hope to get them

—if only our sentry behaved himself in the way he usually did.

Our plans were that I was to be the first one out. Howard would follow, then Mac. Once started it was to be each man for himself. We were to make straight for the fences and get through as quickly as we possibly could. Suddenly it was nine o'clock—the eventful moment had arrived. I grabbed Frank and wished him goodbye. He held me tight for a moment as he returned my farewell. Then he let go and fell back.

We held our bags in our hands and waited, our nerves keyed up to breaking-point. Yes, the guards were coming from the guard house. They came along as they always came, straggling and slowly, carrying their arms just anyhow. They were passing our position, and we strained our eyes to see if our friend was among them. He was—and we held our breaths as we watched to see if he was to take over Number Two post as usual. He stopped, and the rest of the guard moved on to the next post. I don't know how long we waited after that. Each moment seemed like an hour as we crouched there, gripping our bags, waiting and watching for our sentry to make his usual evening stroll.

At last he moved. The instant he was round the corner, I made a dash for the fence. There was no turning back now. I fell on my chest, scrambled under the first wire, the second, the third. I saw the other two following, and streaked across the space to the fourth and fifth fences. I was through! Howard and Mac followed. We were all through! Shaking all over, we walked quickly until we were a little way away from the camp. Then we sat down to regain our breaths and to see if everything was still quiet behind us.

All was still. Our guards had not seen us. For the moment, at any rate, we were free. Now our fate depended upon ourselves. The immediate world was against us, and our lives were in our own hands. If we were to win through to safety, we should have need of all the courage and grit and determination that we possessed.

After a few minutes, we got up and made our way towards the main road. Just before we reached it we heard voices. A party of Japanese soldiers, sounding rather drunk and disorderly, was on its way back to camp. We kept perfectly still

D

until the party was by, then we pushed on through the trees until we reached the main road.

Here we had a sudden fright. A torch was flashed in our faces, and for a second or two our hearts stood still. Two Malays were on their way home. Howard spoke up quickly.

" Tedda chuck-up Nippon," he said, which meant, " Don't tell Nippon." And one of the Malays answered in English : " All right." We did not stop for further conversation, but pushed on with extra speed.

Soon we had to leave the main road and cross a rice field in order to reach the jungle. The going was tough, for there was much fallen timber lying about, and there were creeks to be crossed. One of these proved to be much deeper than I expected, and I found myself up to the chest in muddy water. We all got very wet before we were over it. However, we struggled on, climbing over the fallen trees and wading through the rice pools until at last we came to the fringe of the jungle.

It would have been good to rest here for a while, but we did not dare to do so, for workers in rice fields are often on the job before dawn. So we moved on for some way into the jungle, and then found a spot where we could stay for the remainder of the night. I opened my bag to get a change of clothes—I had kept a shirt and a pair of shorts in reserve— refraining from wearing them for anything even though my everyday gear was in rags—especially for use in my escape. Getting my garments out, I came upon the parcel which Joo Meng had left for me that afternoon. It contained a dozen rissoles and a little fried rice, and the food proved most acceptable. We each ate a little rice and a rissole and drank a little of the water we had brought in our water-bottles. Then we changed our clothes, hung up our wet ones to dry, and settled down for a well-earned sleep. We decided to sleep in relays, leaving one man always on the watch for safety's sake.

The next morning we were up very early, and, having made sure that we had left no tell-tale marks behind us, we set out to follow a jungle trail into the unknown.

It was very quiet in the jungle. The atmosphere was humid, and visibility very bad. We only got glimpses of the sun from time to time, as the trees formed a tunnel of interlocking branches over our heads. Occasionally snakes slithered across the path, startling us at first, but we soon become used to them and they disappeared quickly into the undergrowth on each side of the primitive track. From time to time, too, we came across bands of monkeys. They swung on the vines from tree to tree, chattering among themselves as they watched our progress into their territory.

As we trudged along, we whistled a little, for we felt light-spirited and exhilarated by our freedom. My plan was to head south-west on a compass bearing of 197 degrees until we reached a place called Seroi. From there we would turn south-east, cross a mountain range, and make for Lahad Datu, a coastal village, where we hoped to get transport to take us to the island of Tawi Tawi, where we should find the Guerilla Unit of which Joo Meng had told me. This was my first plan, but should anything go wrong with it, I had an alternative, which was to get back within a wide circle of the aerodrome site, make contact again with Joo Meng, who would get a boat for us, in which we could get down river to the sea and head for Tawi Tawi.

We took a rest period after we had walked for some time, and sat down to a meal of rissoles and rice and water. While we were sitting happily together we suddenly felt something on our legs, and found that we were being raided by leeches. We had the devil of a job getting them off, and even when we were walking on again, we were still bothered with them. Howard gave us a fright, too, soon after this, by thinking that he heard a movement in the undergrowth. We stopped and listened, but could hear nothing, and the light was too dim for us to see much. We moved on, then again there came a noise, and once more we stopped, all of us gripping our parangs. I had my revolver, too, at the ready. The sweat poured off us from sheer fright as we stood waiting. But nothing happened, and again we walked on.

On we went, climbing over the fallen trees which here and there blocked the track. Some of them were twelve feet in diameter, but we usually had to get over them, for the undergrowth on each side was mostly too thick to get through. There were small streams and shallow pools, too, to be crossed, and now and again one of us would slip and fall and have to be hauled on to his feet again. As we walked, we talked of the camp, wondering what was happening there and if Hosijimah knew yet of our escape. Apart from the crushed grass where we had squeezed through the fences, we felt confident that we had left no tracks behind by which we could be followed, and as long as we stayed deep in the jungle we knew we were fairly safe from the Japs, at any rate, for they hated it and never went into it if they could possibly avoid it. Our danger of recapture would come when we reached the cultivated areas near the coast.

But though we felt fairly safe from human beings, we had still the jungle dangers to combat, and we decided to spend that next night up in a tree. We found one in which it would be possible to go to sleep without falling through the branches, and climbing it we made ourselves as comfortable as possible and slept after a fashion, though when we awoke in the morning we were sore and cramped and still tired.

We now found ourselves on the edge of a mangrove swamp, and were soon wading up to our waists in slimy water, which hid long grass reeds, reeds that cut our legs as we tried to push through them. It was a ghastly terrain to negotiate. The mud had a horrible smell, and occasionally one of us would be tripped up by a hidden root and plunge face foremost into it. Mosquitoes added to our sufferings, buzzing about us in millions. What with them and the sharp-bladed grass, our bodies were soon bleeding all over. The foliage was thick overhead, shutting out all sight of the sky and most of the daylight, too. As we knew that there were crocodiles and snakes hidden in these swamps, it can be imagined what a nightmare our passage through this one was.

At last we struggled out of the slime and found our feet on hard ground. We pushed on slowly, then suddenly, right across our path, we came upon a huge black snake which must have been from fifteen to twenty feet when uncoiled. There it lay, curled up in front of us, and we stopped abruptly, frozen with horror. There was no time to lose, and I jerked my revolver from its case and fired at it, fortunately killing it instantly.

There was a combined sigh of relief from all of us as we realised that, for the moment, that danger was over.

When we stopped for our meal, Mac scratched about in the undergrowth and found a few pieces of dried bark with which, after much effort and some swearing, we got a fire going. Soon we had hot rice and corn ready, and we managed also to dry off our damp clothes. That night we again slept in the trees, though not very happily, for the thought of such snakes as the one we had encountered hardly made for restful slumber.

Water vines in this part of the jungle were plentiful, which was very helpful for us. All we had to do was to break a vine and water flowed from it, not very quickly, but fast enough to enable us to fill our bottles and get a good drink. We continued to move on slowly, on this the third day of our escape, none of us feeling too good by this time. Soon we came to another river. It was wider than any of the other streams we had crossed, but a tree overhung it, and climbing up, we swung ourselves over, one at a time, by means of a long slender branch—only to find that we should now have to get through another mangrove swamp. We had to get through it somehow, so in we went, slipping and falling in the evil-smelling mud, assaulted again by mosquitoes as we struggled across to the farther side of it.

By lunch time that day we had had enough. We remembered Hosijimah's words : " If we don't get you the jungle will," and we realised that we could not go on much longer in this exhausting manner. Tired, miserable, hungry, and sore, we sat down to talk things over, and after some discussion, we decided to scrap our first plan, and try to carry out the alternative one—to head north, skirt round the aerodrome site, and get help from Joo Meng. It was a relief to have come to some decision, and with the help of the compass we started off on a northward course.

After travelling all day we came eventually upon the main road. It was dusk when we reached it, and not far up it, standing in a little group, were some natives. They appeared to be quite bewildered, and their eyes were full of fear, as we went up and spoke to them. Howard asked them whereabouts on the road we were, and they said that we were at the fifteen-mile peg. They told us that the Japanese were looking for us, and went up and down the road searching every day. It was lucky for us that we did not come upon the road until dark.

There was a cottage not far off, and we made our way to it and asked for food. The people there looked us up and down as if they could not believe their eyes. It was obvious that they were very frightened, and we realised only too well the danger our presence might mean for them. But, in spite of their fear, they gave us food, fish, eggs, fruit, and cooked rice, and having thanked them gratefully, we marched on still farther north until we reached a pool on the edge of the jungle, where we bathed and washed our clothes. We then sat down and had a really good feed and a good sleep.

Early the next morning we took to the jungle again. In this part of it the wild life was rather different from that which we had encountered when we were pushing to the south-west. There were many more birds about, and the monkeys were man-size. There were, however, still plenty of leeches and mosquitoes to attack us as we moved along. Soon we came to what were known as the Sago Swanps, which were even worse than the mangrove swamps. The turgid water was sometimes shoulder-high, and, in addition to snakes, there were many huge crabs to be avoided. To add to our troubles, Mac's boots had given out, and his feet became so sore that I wrapped my puttees round them. The poor kid was in great pain, it was as much as he could do to limp along. Howard seemed fairly all right, though rather discontented at the slow progress we were making. But that could not be helped—the only thing to do was just to keep plodding on.

Our gear now became a great burden to us. It was constantly wet, and so heavy that we had to discard most of it, since in these swamps we could not keep it dry. After the Sago swamps, we came to more mangrove ones, and knew that we were getting near the main river. This added a new terror to our lives for it would certainly mean crocodiles. Wild boars and civet cats were also known to inhabit this part of the jungle, and it was necessary to be on the alert all the time. Conditions were really almost impossible, and looking

back upon it all now it seems to me a miracle that I am alive
to tell the tale. The nerves of all three of us were strained to
breaking-point, and it was a constant struggle to keep our
self-control.

We came to the river. It was very wide, and we did not
know how we were going to get across it. We sat down to
cool our feet in the water, and while we sat there we saw a
native boat coming towards us. Howard called out to its
occupants to come and help us, but they were too scared to
come near and made off at top speed. After a while we
decided to swim for it, and wrapping our remaining gear up
in a ground sheet we waded into the river, and paddling and
swimming arrived at length on the other side, where, having
found a suitable spot, we rested for the night.

All went well until about midnight, when we were awakened
by a frightful screeching noise in the trees overhead. Jumping up in a fright, we saw, in the moonlight two large orang-
utans out on a midnight spree. We got our parangs and the
revolver ready in case of trouble, but as they kept themselves
to themselves, we did the same and left them alone. But there
was no more sleep for us that night. We were too scared to
blink so much as an eyelid, and as soon as daylight came
we got on our way again.

Things were looking very grim for us by this time. We were
very short of food and quite out of smokes, and soon we
found ourselves once more in thick slimy mud. Howard cut
a couple of long sticks so that, holding on to them, we could
help to pull each other along. The going here was so hard that
we had to stop and rest several times, and when at last we
crawled out of the sticky patch we were all exhausted and
smothered in mud from head to toe.

Close by was another river, even wider than the other one
had been. We had a good bath and clean up in it, and I even
managed to shave myself after a fashion, though why I
worried to do it in the circumstances I do not know. While
we were resting after our bath, another native boat came
along. In it was a Phillippino man and his young son, and to
our great joy, they stopped. That was our happiest moment
since our escape, and our tiredness and terror were forgotten

as the boat drew up beside us. Its owner spoke excellent English and greeted us warmly, asking if he could help us. Our first requests were for a drink of water, something to eat, and a good cigarette, and to our delight all three of these things were produced at once, as though by magic, by this new-found friend.

The Philippino knew all about our escape. He told us that search parties went out daily to look for us. Which of us, he asked, was Wallace? Wallace was the wanted man. I felt a little sick as I listened to him, visualising what my fate might be if I fell again into enemy hands. I knew too much, and knowing too much about the Japanese was not healthy. I thought grimly that it would be better to die in the jungle than be captured again by the Japs.

Our new friend told us to get into his canoe, and he would take us to a somewhat safer place than the spot we were in now. We piled in, and I sat in the stern, keeping a wary eye upon the man, just in case he intended to betray us. But the precaution was not necessary. He proved to be a real friend in need, and having paddled us to a place which it was very unlikely that the Japs would visit, he warned us to move well back from the river bank, and then went off to get us food.

In almost no time at all he was back again, bringing with him cooked rice and fish, and—joy of joys!—hot coffee! A gift from the gods indeed! He said that he would be along with more food later, and then left us to relax over a meal for the first time since we had scrambled under the fences.

It seemed a wonderful feast to us, better even than the one we had had at Christmas because now we were all so very hungry. Our friend was as good as his word, and came back later that day, with more fruit and fish and rice and coffee. I shall never forget his goodness to us. We were hunted men, and with a price on our heads. He ran a terrible risk in helping us, yet he did it, just for the sake of three suffering specimens of humanity.

We slept well that night. When I awoke I felt much refreshed. Howard and Mac were up before me. They were down on the river bank, where Howard was trying to do a

spot of fishing. He had caught one fish, and was trying to get
two more so that we might each have one for dinner. During
our mid-day meal, we had a discussion about our future
moves. Mac was not happy about the slow progress we were
making, and wanted us to push on then and there, swimming
down the river until we got to Joo Meng's house, and then
getting him to find a boat for us. I wanted to get to Joo
Meng, too, but my idea was to go slowly, keeping well away
from roads and river, even if it did mean wading through
swamps and scrambling over fallen timber. Howard did not
say much, but I could see that he agreed with Mac. Neither of
them felt like going back again to our former painful method
of progress.

" I don't see why it couldn't be done," Howard said, but
I refused to be a party to such a foolhardy plan.

" Swimming down the river in broad daylight and landing probably under the very eyes of the Japanese sentries, is
much too risky," I told them. " They are bound to be watching the river as well as the roads, and we should be almost
certain to run right into them. I'm sure my way is the only
possible way for us, even if it does mean hard going and takes
a long time."

We argued about it more or less all that day, Mac doing
his best to persuade Howard that his way was best. The next
morning the discussion started up again. The river was tidal,
and Mac wanted us to swim down on the next out-going tide,
pushing our gear in front of us as we had once before in
crossing a wide stretch of water. In vain I argued with him.
I reminded him that there might be crocodiles, even an odd
shark or two, that we should be open to observation from the
air, as well as from both banks of the river, that we might
meet natives who would betray us for the sake of a possible
reward. I was agreeable to making for the aerodrome and
Joo Meng, but I was determined to keep under cover, no
matter how hard the going or how long it might take.

Howard at last gave in to Mac's persuasions, and the two
decided that on the morrow they would go their own way,
leaving me to follow mine. I was very worried and unhappy
about it, but there was nothing I could do. I had no authority

over them, and all my arguments were useless. We spent the
rest of the day sorting out our gear. They packed theirs in a
ground sheet; I still had my pack, and I stowed my things
into that. There was no ill feeling between us. We stayed
good friends, but we had all three made up our minds, and
their way was different from mine.

The next day was the eighth of May, 1943, and I woke up
feeling sick at heart at the thought of travelling on alone.
Before setting off, I appealed to my companions once more
to listen to reason, but they were both determined to take the
easier way of floating down the river on the out-going tide.
There was nothing for it, but to leave them to it, and
shouldering my pack I moved off into the jungle alone.

" Well, good luck ! And for God's sake be careful," I called,
as I walked away.

I made my way slowly along the bank of the river, keeping under cover all the while. I climbed over fallen trees,
wormed my way through tangled undergrowth, ploughed
through mud-holes. The going was tough, but I was sure that
I was doing the right thing. During the afternoon, while I was
resting under a tree on the river bank, I saw Howard and Mac
drift by on the tide. I waved to them as they passed, and they
waved back, but as I watched them disappear in the distance,
I suddenly experienced an overwhelming feeling of dismay. I
thought :

" If I can see them so well, so can other people," and if I
could have got near them, I think I should have started
arguing with them again, so strong was my premonition of
disaster. But they were out of sight, round a bend of the
river, and I could do nothing but walk on.

I had to cross many streams, which further delayed my
progress, since I had to wrap my pack up in a ground sheet
and push it before me as I swam across to the other side. On
one of these crossings, I packed the sheet badly, with the
result that the bag became full of water and sank. This was
a terrible catastrophe, for the bag not only contained my
clothes, but my compass, binoculars, maps, camera, diary,
revolver, and two hundred dollars as well. I dived again
and again to try to recover my lost treasure, but I could find

nothing but mud, and at last was obliged to give up the effort to retrieve it.

This was a real tragedy, and I felt really brokenhearted. It was as though my whole world had collapsed about me. Not only was I alone, but I was without food and clothes and money. However, it was no good to stay there crying about it, so I went on.

I spent a most uncomfortable night. Apart from all the troubles of the day, I was unfortunate in my resting-places. First I sat down on a crab's bed, which did not please either the occupants or me. I moved, and this time I landed on a hidden ants' nest, the inhabitants of which attacked me viciously. Hunting about for something on which to sit I caught sight of what appeared to be a log floating down the river within reach of the bank. I was moving towards it, when suddenly I realised that it was a crocodile. For a moment I stood frozen with horror. Then it occurred to me that the only sensible thing to do was to become unfrozen again and beat it up a tree—which I promptly did.

As I sat there, shivering, with my heart beating a regular tattoo, I thought of Mac and Howard and prayed fervently that they were well away from this monster. During the night, I kept straining my eyes through the darkness trying to see where the creature had got to. It was a great relief, when daybreak came, to find that the unwelcome visitor had gone.

I climbed down my tree and walked on. My back and legs were aching terribly, and my eyes were also giving me a great deal of trouble. But there was nothing I could do about my aches and pains except endure them. I was very thirsty, but there was little I could do about that, either, for the river here, being tidal, was salt and there was no fresh water to be had. I knelt down and with my hand washed my mouth with the salt water, swallowing a tiny trickle, just enough to moisten my throat and slightly relieve its dryness. Then again I plodded on.

The trees were more dense than ever, and I had to climb over more fallen ones than I could keep count of. The ground was slippery and dangerous, and there were masses of tangled roots everywhere, ready to trip me up. I had to go very slowly and take many rest periods, for I felt terribly sick and tired, and my feet and legs were very sore. Life was almost unbearable, but my will to live was still there, and somehow I struggled on.

The next day was May the eleventh, and it found me almost out of the jungle. About a mile ahead was the mouth of the river, and from now on there would be no cover at all. I had to come to some decision as to what to do next. Close by me, I saw two small logs, and it occurred to me that if I tied these together, I could, after dusk, float the rest of the way with the out-going tide. I should have to use my one and only shirt to make the ties, but if I swam it would get wet, anyway, so that would not matter much. I sat down and tied the logs together, then I moved well back from the water to a spot where there was good cover, and lay down for a long rest.

Dusk came, and I felt certain that even if the Japanese had been keeping a watch by the river they would have left by now. They had a terror of jungle animals, which, at this time of day, would be on the prowl. Also, they had bitter enemies in the Dyaks, the tribes who inhabited the hills. These savage men would creep up silently with their blow pipes, and discharge poisoned arrows at any unwary intruder they could find. They had accounted for many of the Japs already, and had instilled into the invaders a very wholesome dread. The time had come for me to set off on this dangerous stage of my journey, and pushing the logs very quietly into the water, I uttered a silent prayer for guidance and protection and started.

The water was cool and soothing, and I enjoyed the sensation of floating gently and easily along. It was necessary, of course, to keep a sharp lookout for lurking crocodiles, or for the upraised fin which would mean a shark, and whenever I came to a bend in the river, I would edge over to the off-side, to get a view of what lay ahead before going farther. But nothing happened to cause me any alarm, and, apart from an occasional arm stroke, made with caution so as not to splash, I had nothing to do but float smoothly with the tide towards my destination.

I had just come to the point—barely recognisable in the dusk—where I intended to leave the water, when suddenly, without any warning, my two logs became water-logged and sank beneath me. I was tired, and taken by surprise I sank with the logs. When I came up again, I was out in the middle of the river, which was almost two miles wide here so near the mouth. Down I went for the second time, swallowing mouth-fuls of water in doing so. When I surfaced once more, I sent up a heart-felt prayer to God to save me, for I felt too utterly exhausted to do anything to save myself. Once more I went under, and when I came to the surface for the third time, I found that one of the logs had come up also, and was close beside me. If ever a prayer was answered surely mine was then! I caught hold of the log, and shut my eyes, too done in to do more than cling to it and let the tide carry me where it would. And by some miracle it brought me to the exact spot where I wanted to get out. I struggled out of the water, and with a murmured prayer of thanks lay down for a little while to recover some of my strength.

But this was no place to rest, and as soon as I could, I scrambled up the bank and found a tree against which I could lean for another breathing-space. Close by I could just distinguish a kind of cabbage-leaf palm, and being des-perately hungry, I moved across to it and picked some, eating it raw. While I was eating, my foot kicked against something on the ground. Picking it up I found to my horror that it was an empty cigarette packet, quite new. Obviously, it must have been thrown down by a Japanese guard, keeping watch on the river at this particular point.

My heart seemed for a moment to stand still. My thoughts flew to Mac and Howard. Had they been able to dodge this trap, or had they been caught? The sentries, if they were sentries, had probably been stationed here all day, and it would have been broad daylight when Mac and Howard had tried to land. My legs would hardly move for tiredness, but I forced myself to journey on. It was essential to get away from this danger spot as quickly as possible.

Keeping away from the road, I headed cautiously for the outskirts of the aerodrome. It occurred to me that in the kitchen erected there for daytime cooking there might be a little rice. Even a mouthful would be a godsend, I was so ravenously hungry. There were native huts built on the verge of the site, and when I came to these I dropped down and crawled on hands and knees, for it was imperative now that I should not be seen by anyone. Joo Meng was the only person I could really trust. While I was crawling I came upon a pool of water. It was fresh water, and I lay down and lapped some of it up like a dog. Finding it was a wonderful piece of luck and I felt much better after I had thus quenched my thirst.

I reached the kitchen safely, but not a grain of rice or of any kind of foodstuff was to be found. Bitterly disappointed, I slipped into one of the large drains that ran round the drome, and crept very carefully past a guard house. I could hear the Japs talking inside it, but as I could not in any case understand what they said, I did not try to listen but pushed cautiously on. Creeping as stealthily as if I were some animal stalking its prey, I made my way through the familiar paths of the jungle round the site, until I got close to a house that I knew well. I listened carefully for voices within it, just in case Japs were visiting the house. Then, hearing no sound, I called out very softly:

" Joo Meng, Mari Sini Lacass! Joo Meng, come here quick !"

Then I moved back from the house into cover, for I was taking no risks.

After a moment or two, the door opened, and a face I knew peered out. I called again, as softly as before, and Joo Meng came out of the house, closed the door behind him, looked both ways to make sure no one was in sight, and then came across to the place where I was hiding. I came out from cover, and we embraced each other like long-lost brothers. He poured out questions upon me; one of them was:

" Hungry?"

I told him that I was starving, and he put his arm round me and helped me into the house. Some of his friends were there, and realising at once what was happening, promptly went outside and took up guard positions round the house, leaving Joo Meng to see to my physical needs. I had nothing on but a pair of bathing trunks—my only possessions at the moment—and it did not take him long to see how cut and bruised I was. He put some water on to boil, and then set to work to feed me.

I asked him if he had seen Howard or Mac, but he had not, and had heard no news of them. When the water boiled, he set to work to bathe my tired body. He was shocked at the scars it bore, not all of which had been caused by the cuts and bruises I had sustained during the escape. Many were marks from tortures devised by the Japanese. When he had bathed me, he gave me fresh clothes, a cigarette, and a nice pillow, and lying down I fell immediately into a deep and refreshing sleep.

The next morning I was awakened early, to find that Joo Meng and his friends had stayed awake to keep guard over me all through the night. They told me then that there had been great trouble in the camp when our escape became known. Joo Meng had been in touch with Frank, who had told him all about it. I should be told all the news later, I was promised. The urgent thing at the moment was to get me into a safer place. I was taken to a hideout deep in thick bush, where I was given breakfast, provided with some books to read, and told to keep quiet and rest.

Joo Meng and his friends went back to the house to get their own breakfasts, but Joo Meng returned very soon to keep his promise to tell me all the news. He told me that the Japs had been hot on our trail. Every day search parties had been sent out to every place where it was thought we might have been hiding. On three occasions Joo Meng had been placed in charge of a party of Chinese, commandeered to join in the hunt. The Japs had asked him where he thought we might be, and knowing that we had not intended to go anywhere near it, he had suggested the Twenty Mile Peg. The Japs went with the party until they reached the edge of the jungle, then they sent Joo Meng and the Chinese in to search, while they stayed outside. As I have said, they were never keen to go inside the jungle.

" We went in about a mile," Joo Meng said. " Then we sat down and smoked for the rest of the day. When it was time to come out, we made ourselves look the worse for wear, and told the Japanese that you were not there."

I felt overwhelmingly grateful to him. When I said that my bathing trunks were my only possession, I had forgotten one thing. I had a wrist watch, a Kesan Calendar Watch. It had stopped the day before when I had got so nearly drowned, but it was the only thing I had, so I took it off my wrist and gave it to him as a keepsake.

Joo Meng gave me in return a solid ivory cigarette holder to keep in remembrance of him. Lighting a cigarette which he also gave me, I then related the gist of our adventures since he had last seen me. He was amazed at what we had endured, and thought that it was just one miracle after another that we had survived.

" How you are still alive I just don't know," he said.

" I don't either," I told him. " But I'm terribly worried about Howard and Mac. If only I could get news of them I might feel better."

Joo Meng went off after that, and I fell asleep. How long I slept I don't know, but the next thing I knew was Joo Meng shaking me awake. His face was very grave, and one glance at it told me that he had something dreadful to tell me. Before he began he made me drink a little brandy he had brought. Then, lighting a cigarette for me, he looked at me compassionately, and said :

" Wal, the news I have to give will make you very sad. It grieves me to tell you, but you will have to know. Howard Harvey and Daniel MacKenzie are dead."

He stopped and looked at me, and after a pause I said :

" Please go on," and he continued his story.

" They arrived at the mouth of the river, just near where you got out of the water, while it was still daylight, and found five Malays standing watching them. They asked the Malays if they could find a boat. The Malays said that they would and two of them went off, while the other three stayed with Howard and Mac, but instead of getting a boat they returned with six Japanese soldiers. Howard and Mac were tied up and taken away to a lonely spot where the Japanese fired a complete clip of cartridges into Howard. Howard died immediately, and then the Japanese fired another clip into Mac. Mac didn't die at once, and the Japanese clubbed him to death with the butt of their rifles."

There was another silence. Then Joo Meng added:

" I am so sorry, Wal. Oh, why didn't they take your advice and stay with you?"

I sat speechless for a long time. Words would not come, and I felt dazed and ill. I thought of the many dangers we had been through together, the snakes, the death swamps, the hunger, and the pains we had endured. And now, because of an unwise, impatient decision, they were both dead.

Of the many bitter hours I had experienced since I had been taken prisoner, I think that hour in the jungle hide-out was the bitterest of all.

E

CHAPTER V

ON BERHALA ISLAND

J o o M e n g left me to my grief, and disappeared into the jungle. During the day I was visited by a little woman, who looked after Joo Meng and his friends. She brought with her some nourishing food, some cigarettes, and some magazines for me to read. She was a frail-looking little thing, and as I ate I thought how wonderfully brave she was to take this risk. She was certain to lose her life if the Japs ever got to know that she had fed me. While she sat watching me eat, she tried to talk to me in broken English. It was hard to understand what she said, but I gathered that she was expressing her sorrow for me at having lost my two companions, and that she knew I was going to be all right.

It was at dusk, just twenty-four hours since I had struggled out of the river, that Joo Meng came to visit me again. He asked me how I had passed the day, and then told me what he had been doing. I thought he had been at work, but I learnt now that he had given work a miss for the day, and, instead, had been into Sandakan to see some of his friends who worked for the Underground. He learnt from them that on May the seventeenth, a "Kompit" was leaving for Tawi Tawi, and that arrangements were being made for me to go with it.

I felt jubilant at this news, and was quite prepared to face the waiting period. I asked what a Kompit was, and Joo Meng told me that it was a large sailing boat. He also told me that the Japanese had intensified their search for me. Houses, shops, and cars were being examined, paddy fields were being trampled down by the numbers of soldiers combing through them, even fallen tree trunks and logs were being turned over, in case I should be hiding underneath. I felt guilty as I listened, knowing that I was putting the lives of Joo Meng and his friends in jeopardy by letting them shelter me. Joo Meng sensed what I was feeling and told me not to worry. Every possible precaution was being taken, and as long as I did exactly as I was told, things would be all right.

The next few days passed very slowly. From my hiding-place I could hear the lorries driving up and down the aerodrome site, I could hear the guards screaming " Speedo," and the sounds of work going on through all the hours of daylight. It was nerve-racking lying there, and the slightest rustle in the undergrowth from some bird or animal made my blood run cold. Meals were brought to me three times a day, I felt terribly guilty, eating food which I knew my friends needed themselves. But none of them ever seemed to grudge it. Without exception they were all as kind and generous and sympathetic as they could be.

During these days of waiting, Joo Meng brought me letters from some of my mates back in the camp, who had entrusted them to him, knowing that, if anyone knew where I was it would be he. I was very surprised to get them, but they were very welcome. I also received visits from Sergeant Abin and Detective Lagan of the Sandakan police, and from a man named Moo Sing, who had the responsibility of arranging my passage on the boat on the seventeenth. This man was a Philippino-Chinese, and a staunch member of the Underground Movement.

At last May the seventeenth arrived. I was on pins and needles as I waited for the evening, when the journey was to begin. Joo Meng was accompanying me as far as Sandakan. We had our evening meal and then set off. It was very dark, with clouds hiding the moon for which we were grateful. We stole cautiously along a narrow, winding, jungle trail, brushing away overhanging branches and stepping over fallen tree stems here and there. Once Joo Meng stopped abruptly and stood taut, listening. I could not hear a thing, but froze in my tracks when he did. We stayed put in that position for fully ten minutes before at length he beckoned me on.

At last we came to a water-way, where we found Moo Sing and Detective Lagan waiting in a boat. They told me to get in and lie flat on the bottom. Joo Meng climbed in after me and took up a position in the stern. We pushed off and moved quietly down the river. The oars had been padded so as to make no noise. In the silence I heard, far away, the scream of a deer which was being dragged under water by a crocodile. After what seemed an eternity, we reached the mouth of the river, where we waited a little while to make sure that there were no patrol boats about. All was clear, so a square sail was hoisted and as there was a slight breeze we were soon heading out to sea.

When we had gone far enough, down came the sail, and fishing lines were thrown into the water, just in case any enemy was watching. The lines had no bait on them, but that did not matter, for it was not fish that we were after. Hour after hour we waited in the darkness, but the Kompit did not arrive at the appointed place. Something had gone wrong, and at last, since dawn would soon be breaking, we were obliged to turn round and go back to the jungle hide-out.

I was bitterly disappointed, and very anxious, too, for I knew what a risk my friends were running on my behalf. Moreover, I was again eating their scanty supplies of food. I could do nothing, though, except wait as patiently as I could. I was helped by receiving two more letters that same day, one from Frank, and one from Lieutenant Charlie Wagner who was imprisoned on Berhala Island, a small island quite near to the mouth of the river down which we had gone last night. Charlie's letter said that he had heard of my escape, and told me to get to Berhala Island as soon as I could. There a Corporal Korum would meet me and guide me to a place of safety where I could wait until I received further directions. Corporal Korum, it appeared, was in the local police force and was another Underground worker for the Allies.

Joo Meng had taken another day off from work and had gone into Sandakan to make enquiries about the mishap of the previous night. He came to see me after dark, as happy and cheerful as if nothing had gone wrong. He brought with him a friend of his named Jonnie Funk, who was also something to do with the Underground. Joo Meng had been to see Dr. Taylor and he brought me a parcel from him which contained clothes, toilet gear, and money, and a letter telling me to keep my chin up. All these letters and gifts brought me near to tears. Indeed, the kindness I received was almost embarrassing, since I was helpless to return it in any way. All I could do was to write back and say " Thank you."

Again came a time of waiting in suspense. One night I heard the Japs visiting Joo Meng's home. I was terribly worried, but I dare not go any nearer to find out what was happening. I just had to wait, sweating with anxiety, until they had gone. But it seemed that all they wanted was to get him to cook some eggs for them. What a relief it was when I learnt that it was only that!

I had another letter from Frank, telling me that patrols were still going out daily hunting for me. Wild rumours about me, he said, were going through the camp. The latest was that I had been shot in the right shoulder and had died from starvation near the Eight Mile peg. I had a letter, too, from Sergeant McAlister Blain. Blain, in civilian life, represented Darwin in the House. He enclosed a note addressed to the Honourable Frank Forde who, at that time, was Minister for the Army, asking me to deliver it when I reached Australia. It was cheering to know that one person, at least, believed that I should be successful in my dash for freedom!

I became ill while I was waiting for the Underground to arrange another attempt at escape. My throat grew very sore and an abcess developed which caused me great pain. I could eat nothing and could only sip water with difficulty. I was more worried than ever, finding myself in this state. I was scared that I might be going in for malaria, for, as everywhere in the jungle, mosquitoes were about in millions. If I were to go down with a bad attack of malaria, it surely would mean the end.

On the thirtieth of May another letter came from Charlie Wagner, telling me that everything was in hand, and all pre-

parations had been made for my journey. Everyone became
happy and excited again. We waited for darkness, then we
had our tea and set off, creeping as stealthily as before along
the trail until we came to the river and the boat in which our
two accomplices were waiting. Joo Meng had brought along a
supply of fruit and other food, and there were in the boat
a pillow, two blankets, and some magazines for me. We set off
as before making our way down the stream and out to sea.
This time, though, we did not wait about for any Kompit,
but headed straight for Berhala Island. I ought, I suppose, to
have been on top of the world, but I was feeling too bad to
be happy. My throat was giving me hell, and my head felt as
though someone was hitting it with a sledge hammer. I looked
back at Sandakan, and thought of all the deaths and suffering
that had taken place—and were still taking place—there. And
I thought of two people who should have been with me in
that boat.

We stopped off the north-west tip of Berhala Island. Joo
Meng landed first, and carried my gear up the beach. Then
he came back for me, and gave me my instructions. I was to
go a little further inland and hide, and when I saw a man
walk by alone on the beach I was to give a little "Mee-ow"
like a cat. If the lone man was Corporal Korum, the mew
would be answered by another, and I was then to make
myself known to him, and he would see to the next move.

Joo Meng squeezed my hand tightly as we said goodbye.
It was a parting of the ways, and I think we both knew that
we should never see each other again, though Joo Meng said
as he wished me luck " Don't forget I shall see you in Australia when the war's over," and I responded with a heartfelt,
" God bless you, Joo Meng, you and yours till we meet again."
We embraced like brothers, then he turned away and ran
down to the boat, which soon disappeared into the darkness.

I moved back from the beach as he had told me to do,
and sat down behind a tree. As I sat down, I felt suddenly
faint, and stretched out flat on the ground. The next thing
I knew it was daylight. I had fallen asleep and missed the
corporal, and all the carefully-laid plans had gone awry.

I felt awful about it. So much risk and trouble had been

taken on my behalf and I had failed in the one small thing
I had been asked to do. The only thing that gave me any
comfort was that the abcess in my throat had burst, and for
the first time for days I was out of pain. That did make me
feel a little happier, and after a while I pulled myself together
and got up to survey the situation.

The prison camp, I knew, was down at the other end of
the island, so there was not a great chance of running into any
Japanese guards at this end, though I had, of course, to be on
my guard all the time. In front of me was the beach, and
behind me a long mountain range. A single track wound up
towards the summit of the range, and I set out to follow it. It
led me through light jungle and brought me out at last at the
northern end of the island, about five hundred feet above sea
level. From this position I could see a long way, and I realised
that the range ran along the whole length of this somewhat
egg-shaped island. The prison camp, I knew, was somewhere
at the southern end, and in the camp was Charlie Wagner,
the man with whom I needed to get in touch. I decided to
walk along the ridge of the mountains, and see how near I
could get to the camp without exposing myself to the enemy.

I stepped out, walking as quickly as it was possible to do,
and after some time came to a dead end. At the dead end was
a " Trig Point ", which interested me for although I could not
at first see it, I felt sure that there must be some negotiable
pathway down the steep cliff. I couldn't imagine that the
point would have been placed here, if the only way to reach it
was by walking all the way from the other end of the mountain ridge. So I hunted about in the undergrowth, and
presently came upon a little-used track which led downwards.
Following it, I came almost at once in sight of the quarantine
station, which was, as I knew, the prison camp.

It would now be necessary to go very carefully, and to
travel as light as possible, so I hid my new kit and set off,
thinking, I remember, that it was rather ironical that I who
so lately had escaped from one prison camp should now be
heading for another one. Getting down the steep slope was
not as easy as I had expected. There were deep holes here
and there, some of them full of water, and occasionally a

fallen tree had to be negotiated. But bit by bit I made my way down, going as quietly as I could and stopping at every bend to peer cautiously round before turning it.

At one of the bends, I caught sight of a guard, leaning against a tree, taking cover from the sun. I stopped short in my tracks and considered what to do next. The barbed wire fence, I saw, was only about thirty yards away, so I slumped on to my hands and knees and slipped as silently as a cat into the undergrowth. Then, making a detour to avoid the guard, I crawled quietly and steadily right up to the fence.

Just inside, three prisoners were sitting talking together. I broke softly into their conversation.

" Don't look round," I said. " Keep just as you are for a moment or two, then will one of you, please, move off quietly without showing any concern, and bring Charlie Wagner here to the fence? Tell him Wallace is just outside."

They did just as I told them. One of the men got up and moved off in a leisurely manner, and a minute or two later, the others followed him, showing equal unconcern.

I waited, and presently Charlie appeared. He was carrying a book, and sitting down he opened it and pretended to read. Under cover of this manoeuvre he talked to me in a whisper.

" How are you? Are you all right? Are you hungry?" he asked.

I replied in a whisper as low as his own that I was all right, but that I was certainly very hungry. He pointed out the guard positions to me and warned me to be very careful. Then, noticing my bare feet, he asked what size boots I took. I told him I took size eight, and explained that I had lost most of my clothes. He then directed me to go back up the track for about eighty yards and to wait there under cover. He would be out after dinner with a wood-chopping party, he said, and he would see me then.

Then, shutting his book, he got to his feet and strolled away.

I turned round, and crawling again on my hands and knees I made my way back up the track as he had instructed me to do. In about half an hour the working party came out

and wound its way up the hill nearly to the spot where I was
hiding. The guards who escorted it went and sat on a fallen
tree trunk, where they stayed, smoking and talking, confident
that no one could escape from a jungle island or otherwise
disturb their peace of mind. Charlie moved a little away from
the other prisoners, pretending to urinate, and I gave the
agreed signal of a soft mew. He came over close to where I
was crouched, bringing with him three other officers, Captain
Ray Steel, Lieutenant Rex Blow, and Lieutenant Miles Gillon.
They asked me if I had any gear, and when I said I had just
a little and told them where I had planted it, Charlie and
Rex went off quite unconcernedly and brought it back near to
where we were. I was amazed at the way the guards allowed
them to wander about. Had we tried to move about like that
during working hours at Sandakan, we should certainly have
been for it!

While they were gone, I talked to Ray and Miles, telling
them what had happened to " B " Force since it had left
Singapore. When Charlie and Rex returned I had to repeat
the story. They were all very disturbed when they heard of
the treatment meted out to us, and shocked at the extent of the
death roll. Charlie took me to a more secluded position, along-
side a running stream, and told me to stay there until it was
dark, when, if I returned to the fence, I would receive something to eat. Then, warning me to be quiet, a warning I did
not need, he went back to the working party.

Slowly the time dragged on. I watched the men returning
to the camp with the logs of wood, I watched the check
parade, the meal parade, and, still later, the final check parade
of the day. I sat where Charlie had left me, hardly moving
an inch, until it was quite dark. Then, getting to my feet, I
crept softly back to the fence.

Charlie was there waiting for me. The first thing he did
was to present me, to my delight, with a pair of size eight
boots. Then he passed over the food he had managed to bring.
While I ate, he told me that the whole camp was going to be
shifted over the water to Sandakan in about a week's time.

" But the whole camp won't be going," he told me. " There
will be seven men short on that roll call." And he explained

that he and Ray, Miles and Rex, together with three other fellows, Sapper James Kennedy, and Privates Jock McLaren and Rex Butler had made plans to escape in the course of the next few days. I was to join the party, and with the help of the Underground, we would all be hidden in the island until a kompit could be procured to take us to Tawi Tawi. It seemed to me that the whole world must have heard of Tawi Tawi, since everybody was heading for it.

Fed and watered and armed with a good supply of smokes, I went back to my stream, where I was able to take a bath. It seemed a fantastic situation, with a Japanese sentry less than a hundred yards away, but there was thick jungle between him and me, and it was the camp he was watching, not looking for an escaped prisoner of whom he knew nothing. A short time after midnight, I heard a slight sound in the undergrowth. I listened with my ear on the ground, and as the sound came nearer, I took the precaution of slipping quietly behind a tree, where I stood motionless, waiting in suspense to find out who or what had caused it. But it was all right. It was Corporal Korum himself who arrived, the Underground worker in the police force whom I had missed on the beach. He had been told of my whereabouts and sent to find me and move me to a safer place higher up the hill. We had to go very quietly indeed to reach it, in one place the track led within fifteen feet of a sentry, and I hardly dared to breathe as we crept past him. But by this time, I was a past master at moving silently, and could move noiselessly even over sticks and dried leaves.

Corporal Korum had chosen a greatly superior position for my next hiding-place. He had even erected a jungle bed in it for my greater comfort. It was made from saplings, tied together with jungle vines and raised about three feet off the ground. I sat down on it, feeling amused at the audacity of it all. There was the camp, just below us, and here was I, the escaped prisoner, making himself extremely comfortable on a bed.

The Corporal sat down beside me, and we talked for a long while. Then we had a feed of fruit and a smoke together, and he went off, leaving me to go to sleep. About half past three, however, I was awakened by another noise. Somebody was coming up the trail, not quietly as Corporal Korum had come, but making row enough to wake the dead. I thought that only a Jap or a madman would dare to make that noise, and tumbled off my bed in a cold sweat. It was a madman— two madmen to be exact. Rex and Miles announced their arrival, asking, in a choice collection of swear words, what on earth I was sleeping on. Then, without giving me time to answer, they dumped a bundle of their gear beside me, telling me to mind it, and shot off.

During the four days of my stay in this particular hiding- place, I had frequent visitors. Sometimes they were friendly police, sometimes one or more of the officers who were plan- ning to escape. This helped considerably in passing the time, which otherwise dragged interminably. Other less welcome visitors were snakes, scorpions, centipedes, and millions of ants and mosquitoes. The snakes, though they frightened me, slipped past quickly, but the mosquitoes were much too friendly and always stayed for a bite !

On June 4th, at 2 a.m. Corporal Korum wandered up to my residence and told me to wake up and keep on the alert, as soon I should have visitors. I sat up and smoked a cigarette to keep myself awake, and while I sat, smoking and thinking and listening, Ray, Rex, Charlie, and Miles, all turned up in a bunch. They had news for me. The camp was being moved to Sandakan the next day, and they would be slipping away to join me that very night. There was a place on the island, Charlie told me, where the Underground workers thought we could all hide in safety until a boat could be found to take us to Tawi Tawi.

This was wonderful news for me. The others had to go back to camp before long, but they left work for me to do. I was to employ myself during the day in shifting all the stores and gear they had collected to a spot much farther up the hill, and then wait up there with it until they came to me after dark. I did as I was told, and during the day moved everything to a position much farther up the hill and hid them near the track, in a place from which, concealed myself, I could watch the movements down in the camp.

I had a good view of them. For the last time, I watched the meal parade and then the check parade. I could see groups of men laughing and talking together and it made me feel sick. In their present camp, it seemed that they had not had too bad a time, but I knew only too well the condtions to which they were going on the morrow. They would be beaten and half-starved, many of them would die—and not from natural causes. It was terrible to sit there looking at them, knowing what I knew and yet unable to do a thing about it.

Darkness gathered. With eyes and ears strained I watched and listened and waited. Yes, coming up the mountain trail were seven figures. To me it seemed as though they made noise enough for a battalion, and their figures silhouetted against the moon up above could easily have been picked off, one at a time, by a sniper. But luckily none was there, and they reached me safely, and we loaded up our gear and set off along a narrow, dangerous track which wound round the side of the mountain.

Presently, when we were well out of sight of the camp, we came to a junction, one path running downhill, and one continuing along the side of the range. Here Charlie Wagner and Rex Blow dumped their own gear, and went with Jock McLaren, Jim Kennedy and Rex Butler, along the downhill trail to make sure that they reached the beach safely. These three were to go by a different boat from the one the rest of us were to take. It had been found necessary to split up the party, and it had been decided that they were to be first away. Ray, Miles, and myself, went on a little farther and then sat down to wait for Charlie and Rex Blow to return. While we were waiting, Ray checked up on the gear to see if we had everything. To our dismay we found that we hadn't. I had lost the ivory cigarette holder which Joo Meng had given me, a loss which could never be replaced, and Ray found that he had dropped a boot—a real give-away, if it should be picked up by the wrong person—and that one of the water-bottles was also missing.

These two losses were serious, and Ray went back along the track to see if he could find the missing articles. When he came back, his face was enough to tell us that he had been unsuccessful, and we were all in a bit of a panic, wondering what would happen if the Japanese should get hold of them. However, one thing was certain, nobody would find them that night, anyway, so we tried to calm down and not worry unduly.

Rex Blow and Charles rejoined us after a while. They were very pleased, for the other three men had succeeded in pinching a small boat down on the shore and were now out at sea.

The place we were in was considered to be fairly safe, and we stayed in it through the night and all the next day. Our meals were not too good that first day. For breakfast we each had a banana and a drink of water, and then nothing else until tea-time, when we filled up with a couple of rissoles apiece and another mug of water. The next day, our banana breakfast was enlivened by a spoonful of sugar, probably pinched at some time from the Japs. We did not dare to light a fire during the day time, for the smoke might have been seen, but when darkness came on the second day, Charlie and Rex fixed up blankets to make a thick screen and then lit a fire which was very cheering. Over the fire they cooked some dried fish and boiled some rice, doing enough to give us a good supper and provide for our meals on the following day.

That night our peace was much disturbed by the barking of a dog, which had apparently sensed our presence. Charlie crept to the edge of a cliff as soon as it was daylight and looked over. The dog was at the bottom, looking up in our direction and barking its head off. Charlie had a revolver and he wondered if he should shoot it. Then his better judgment prevailed and he decided that the risk would be too great. However, it would not be safe to stay where we were in case the dog brought our enemies on our track, so we packed up our goods and chattels and moved on higher up the mountain until we were well away from the wretched animal and it ceased its barking.

Our new position was not at all comfortable. We were now on a steep, rocky slope where it was impossible to lie stretched out at length. We had to sit all the while in a crouching attitude, hard put to it to keep ourselves from slipping. The one good thing about the place was that we could see the sea from it. During the day we saw from our hiding-places behind the boulders, a Japanese patrol boat cruising round the island, and we couldn't help wondering what it was after. Was it perhaps searching for us?

The next morning Charlie, who was both the brains and the organiser of our expedition, told us that we were now to move on to our next address. We were glad to leave our rocky, uncomfortable position, and off we went once more, downhill this time until we reached a stream in a valley. Crossing this, we moved upwards until we came to a really first-class position. It was a space in the middle of waving trees, and it was fitted up with everything we wanted for a pleasant stay. There was a pool of water, to serve us as a bathroom and a wash-tub for our clothes, there was a running stream for drinking purposes, there were branches convenient for clothes-lines, and we had beds which we made from the many saplings which were growing near. As soon as we were settled in, we did our washing and had baths, and then sat down to relax and rest.

After dark, a faint mee-ow was heard from the direction of the stream. Charlie replied to it and then was off like a hare into the undergrowth. He came back bringing with him Corporal Korum and a man named Sallie, who proved to be the officer in charge of the quarantine station. They brought food and good news, and they brought Ray's boot, which was a great relief to everybody, especially to Ray. The water-bottle was never found, but that was not such a dangerous article if found by an enemy as the boot would have been. For water-bottles were often taken when working-parties were out and occasionally lost on quite legitimate excursions.

The food our visitors brought us was a big supply of a Chinese dish called " Marmee." It was a mixture of stewed rice, fish, and prunes, flavoured with salt and pepper and some sort of spice. There were rich vitamins in this food, and it put new life into me. Korum had also a letter for me from Frank, giving me news of the camp. I scribbled a note back, saying that I was safe and had left Sandakan, but did not mention where I was or anything more, in case it should fall into the wrong hands.

We had a wonderful meal that night. Following the

marmee we had some bananas, some vegenite, and, best of all, a cup of tea! Real tea—the first I had tasted since I was taken prisoner. And didn't I enjoy it! No matter in what part of the world he is, an Australian always appreciates a cup of tea, and after such long abstinence from it, it seemed to me like nectar.

We had to spend a week or two in this new hiding-place, and to while away the hours, I suggested to Ray and Rex that we should learn—in my case, rub up the knowledge of the Morse Code, as it might prove useful in our further journey-ings. I always remembered an old sergeant at Georges Heights who often said to us during our training : " You always want to learn signallin'. You never know when it mayn't come in useful. You may be shipwrecked in a desert some day." My companions started to learn with enthusiasm at first, but they soon folded up. They just could not grasp it, though Rex did manage to get as far as V before he gave in. So I practised sending and receiving messages by myself. I had a feeling in my bones, even then, that the accomplishment was going to " come in useful."

On the night of June the twenty-fourth, we saw two figures coming along by the stream. A faint mee-ow sent Charlie off to meet them. It was Korum again, and he brought with him another man whom he introduced to us as " Corporal Quadra of the Guerilla Forces in Tawi Tawi."

We were thrilled—the more so when we learned that Quadra had come to Sandakan in a kompit on a supposed " Trading Mission ", and that he would be leaving for home— that is, for Tawi Tawi—in a few days. This was marvellous news, and our excitement was intense. For the next two days we were all in a whirl, washing and packing and preparing for our departure with as much nervous tension as if we had been a pack of highly-strung girls getting ready for their weddings. I think none of us slept much during our remaining hours in that camp. I know that I spent most of the night lying on my back, gazing up at the stars, thinking about the coming voyage and wondering what fate held in store for us.

CHAPTER VI

WITH THE GUERILLAS ON TAWI TAWI

THE GREAT day arrived—June the twenty-sixth, 1943. We were on tenterhooks all day, fidgeting about and longing for the daylight to go. When the sun was setting and throwing long shadows which would provide a certain amount of cover, Charlie gave us the word to start. " Move," he said, and off we went.

We followed the trail up and over the crest of the mountain, and then headed down towards the sea on the east side of Berhala Island. There was no trail here, but we followed the course of a little stream, going in single file, pushing through the undergrowth on its banks, and sometimes wading knee-deep in the water where the bushes were too thick to get through. On our way down we met Sallie, who had crossed the mountain range just to shake our hands and wish us goodbye and good luck. I gave him a message for Frank when he said farewell to me.

It was dark when we reached the part of the coast chosen for us to await the arrival of a boat. We spread out a little and strained our eyes to scrutinise the water in front of us. We looked to the right, and we looked to the left, but there was nothing that we could see, so we resorted to a signal which had been pre-arranged—the lighting of cigarettes, so that the glow from them might tell the crew of the kompit that we were there. We kept quite still, puffing away, until I was almost sick of smoking. The moon had not yet risen, and we were hoping and praying that it would not rise until we were well

80

away from the island. As time went on, and we still waited, our prayers became almost agonised.

Then, about nine o'clock, a faint mee-ow came drifting to us over the water. Charlie answered, and a few minutes later a big rowing boat loomed up in front of us out of the darkness. The kompit was there. Corporal Quadra, who was in charge of it, neatly and quickly manœuvred it into shallow water, the native crew swarmed out and grabbed our bags, and bundled them, and us, into the boat. Then, just as quietly and quickly as it had come in, the kompit moved away from the shore.

A kompit is a kind of large rowing boat, about twenty feet long with an eight-foot beam. It is shaped at the bow, but the stern is squarish, flattened out to form a table-like platform. It carries a centre mast, on which a sail can be hoisted, and it can be roofed over with attap when desired. As we moved away from Berhala, the sail was hoisted, a good westerly wind filled it, and I, for one, felt full of exultation at the thought that, in spite of Hosijimah and his threats, I had escaped from captivity and was well on my way to further adventures in Tawi Tawi.

Corporal Quadra spoke excellent English, as well as several of the Philippine dialects. He was very excited and jubilant about the venture, for, besides ourselves, the vessel was carrying a cargo of rice, sugar and other commodities which were urgently required in Tawi Tawi. He was very much alive, too, to the risks he was running, and kept a sharp look-out all the time. The darkness was a great protection to us, for we were in the danger zone, and there could always be a stray patrol boat about, armed with weapons and searchlights. He was glad of the favourable wind, which would enable us to get as far away from Berhala as possible before daylight, when possibly an air search might be instituted.

Apart from one slight setback, when the kompit grounded on a sand bank, and all hands had to jump out and get her afloat once more, all went well that first night. It was a perfect night for sailing, the wind cool and fresh and carrying us in the right direction. We escapees slept well. When we awoke, we found that we had covered about ninety miles during the

F

night and were about halfway to our destination. There was a lot of debris and driftwood about, probably from sunken ships. It was a mercy that we had not hit any of it during the night, or the result might have been disastrous.

After lunch the wind dropped, and for a while we were practically becalmed. Quadra, still keeping a keen lookout, saw smoke on the southern horizon, and after watching it for a time, he saw that three ships were coming northward in our direction, and knew that they must be Japanese.

He gave a quick order:

" Lift the covers!" and the crew raised the boards of a false floor which had been designed especially to meet such an emergency. The five of us were put underneath these, flat on our stomachs, and bags of rice and sugar were stacked upon us. The sail was lowered, the attap roof erected, and the crew took to the oars and began rowing leisurely along, looking for all the world as though they were just a few native fishermen, returning home after a day's fishing.

Under the floorboards we were cramped and uncomfortable. We could not talk, and even breathing was not too easy. Quadra spoke to us from time to time, giving us a commentary upon what was happening. About half-past six, the three ships, a cruiser escorting two transports, moved in very close to us, and an officer scrutinised the kompit closely through his binoculars. But he saw nothing suspicious, and the ships continued on their way. Quadra said that he and his crew waved to the officer in friendly salutation, and he waved back.

At about eight, we were released, and if ever I was glad to breathe fresh air, I was glad then! I drew deep breaths of it, and so did the others. We had a cold meal that evening, for it had not been possible to cook anything, and after we had eaten, we sat talking until, one by one, we became drowsy and fell asleep. Unfortunately it was not only the passengers who slept that night. The crew did, too, even the man at the tiller dropping off, and when we woke up in the morning, we found that we had gone round in a circle and were nearly back to the spot we had left twenty-four hours ago.

It was now the twenty-eighth of June. There was still no wind, and the crew rowed for many hours. The sea was as calm as a pond, but after a while it began to rain, increasing in intensity every minute until visibility was practically nil, and we had to stop rowing and drop anchor. Charlie did not intend to let us drift back again, so he took a bearing to Tawi Tawi with his compass, and as soon as the rain stopped he set a course for us to follow. A fresh wind sprang up, and soon we were bowling along in front of it. Presently, Quadra pointed to three objects on the horizon, and said :

" That Tawi Tawi."

But though it looked near, there was still quite a lot of water between us and the island, and we could not make it that day. At nightfall, Charlie checked his compass bearing to make sure there should be no repetition of the drifting of the previous night, not trusting again to the native method of navigation. That, as we had discovered, was usually of the hit-or-miss type. A day more or less on the journey meant nothing to the natives, but to us it might well be vital.

The twenty-ninth of June found us drawing very near to the island. The green trees on it were becoming clearer, and we could distinguish the palm trees from the others. The water was crystal clear, and beneath us we could see the beautifully-coloured coral reefs, in and out of which tropical fish, blue, red, green, purple, in hue, and of many shapes and sizes, darted in search of food. We dropped anchor, and three of the crew waded ashore, returning with a supply of fresh fish, caught in a large fish trap previously set, and a supply of coconuts and sugar canes. The rest of that day we spent bathing and lazing, and enjoying every minute of it.

The next day, June the thirtieth, two months after my escape from the prison camp, was the day on which we were to land. After a light breakfast, we weighed anchor and moved slowly along the coast to a village called Tarawakan, on the north-west of Tawi Tawi. It was market day, and the village was crowded with country people, come in to buy and sell. We expected to land unnoticed, but it seemed that our arrival was expected, and at some signal a crowd of men rushed into the water and surrounded our boat, and carried us and our gear shoulder-high to shore. People came swarming round us, shaking our hands and showing every possible sign of joy at our coming. One would have thought that, after our experiences, we should have been hardened to meet any event, but this unexpected show of loyalty and devotion touched us so deeply that we were overcome by emotion.

Addresses of welcome had been prepared, and were read aloud to us the moment we were on shore, and we were all treated as though we were persons of great consequence. One grey-haired warrior, carrying a spear, grabbed me by the hand and led me from group to group, introducing me as if he had been appointed my personal escort. Food of all desscriptions was showered upon us. It was very welcome, but we could not eat anything like the amount that was lavished upon us, for our stomachs had shrunk owing to the starvation diet of our prison, and, even if we had been able to swallow it, we knew that we must be careful what we ate now. Over-eating in our present condition might easily prove fatal.

Out of the crowds surging around us, an escort of soldiers in various styles of get-up, emerged and led us away. Their weapons were as various as their dress. Some carried rifles, others had spears, bolos, parangs, and krisses. They were all very excited, laughing and cheering, and chattering away in a language which was foreign to all of us. A few of them, though, talked English—or perhaps it would be more accurate to say American—so that we were able to understand a little of what was going on. We were led for several miles along a narrow road through the jungle, and all along it were groups of people waiting to cheer us, and to hand us out food and drink as we passed by. All this hero-worship was quite embarrassing, and if it had been possible for our weather-beaten faces to show our blushes, we should all have been crimson before we came to the end of our triumphal march.

One of our guards had gone ahead to inform the Commander of the Force that we had arrived safely and were on our way to pay our respects to him. Before we reached his headquarters, however, we were delighted to be met by Jock McLaren, Jim Kennedy, and Rex Butler, whom this news had brought out. They had arrived three days ahead of us and were overjoyed to see us, as they had heard that we had been killed in the Macassa Straits. We were all mighty glad to meet again, alive, safe, and well—for the time being.

Soon after our reunion, our guides led us on to a secret track, concealed from the main trail by the heavy, drooping branches of a tree. We followed a narrow path for about half a mile, and then, hidden in the heart of the jungle, we came upon a simple little cottage, the home of Lieutenant-Colonel Alejandro Suarez, P.C., C.C., 125 Inf. Regt. U.S. F. I.P. Here we were greeted warmly by the Colonel himself. He was dressed in the uniform of an American-Philippino, a grey-haired man of about fifty-five, with a pleasant voice and a kindly, smiling face—a fatherly kind of person, I thought, to judge from his appearance.

Ray, who was the senior of our officers, stepped forward and saluted him, and then introduced us all in turn. After these preliminary formalities had been completed, the Colonel took us into his home to have lunch. It was queer to sit at a table again, on proper chairs, with plates and knives, and table-cloths, after the way in which we had eaten our meals during the past two years. It was all so different that I felt a little embarrassed, afraid of exhibiting bad table manners at first. During lunch we exchanged items of news. The Colonel, of course, could tell us something of how the war was going generally, while we could tell him details of what had happened at Singapore, and of the way the Japanese were raping the whole colony, stealing the people's food to send back to Japan, and very nearly allowing the native population to starve. We found that the Colonel knew a great deal about what was going on, thanks to the information supplied through the Underground Service.

After lunch, Rex Blow, Miles Gillon, and I, went for a tour of inspection, escorted by Corporal Quadra. We went south to the other side of the island, our way lying mostly through jungle areas, the trees coming close to the roads on both sides. The sunshine which filtered down through the foliage was brilliant, and we saw birds and butterflies of all descriptions. Attap-built houses were scattered here and there, and bigger dwellings were schools or barracks. These flew the American and the Philippino flags, side by side. It was wonderful to walk about openly like this. Several times I had to reassure myself that it was true, that I was not dreaming.

The next day, Ray and Charlie, as our two senior officers, attended a special conference called by the C.O. After it an Order was posted up, dated July 1, 1943, showing the following appointments :

> Capt. R. E. Steele—Assistant Executive Officer, and Regimental Training Officer.
> Lieut. Charles Wagner—Regimental Intelligence Officer.
> Lieut. Rex Blow—C.O. 1st Battalion.
> Lieut. Miles Gillon—2 i/c 1st Battalion.
> Sgt. W. Wallace—Chief Instructor to the Regiment.
> Sapper James Kennedy, Private Rex Butler, Private Jock McLaren—Assistant Instructors.

As well as being escaped prisoners of the 8st Australian Division, we were also members now of the United States Forces in the Philippines.

Our immediate task was to find accommodation. This we achieved with the help of Corporal Quadra. There were several vacant houses along the one and only roadway, and we selected one near Batu Batu and settled in. The house was of weather-board and attap, and, being on a slope of a hill, was elevated in front, the front veranda being built-in. We were fortunate in being able to obtain beds and cooking gear, together with a cook, a typewriter, and several messengers. We also obtained a mirror, and when I looked in and saw myself for the first time, I wasn't surprised that the people had stared at us. I couldn't think for a moment who it was looking back at me. I had a hell of a beard and my hair looked like an old mop. Of course, I had seen what the others looked like, but it had never occurred to me that I looked the same myself. I looked much worse, in fact, since I had been roughing it longer than any of the others had. The procedure was rather painful, but it wasn't long before we were all looking rather more human again.

While the shaving and hair-cutting was going on, Quadra sat watching, greatly interested in our " New Look." While he watched, he told us something about the island. The jungle was infested by deadly snakes, and it contained, also, wild boars and wild cattle. Monkeys lived in the tree-tops, and there were the usual mosquitoes, scorpions, centipedes and spiders. There were many small rivers, in which crocodiles and sharks appeared from time to time. Fishing was a flourishing industry. Using one method fisherman would sit for hours on a kind of tripod, made from long poles which were stuck in the bed of the river and rose out of the water. The people, also, grew much rice and corn in the fertile regions.

A few days after our arrival it was America's Independence Day, the Fourth of July. It happened, also, to be my daughter's birthday. She was thirteen that year, and in my heart I sent her my fervent wishes for a very happy birthday. We all joined in the celebrations which were held in the local school's grounds. Tables were laid out, and there was abundance of food, rice, fish, fruit, together wtih a little poultry and pork. At the end of the banquet there were speeches, during the afternoon there was cock-fighting—a favourite sport on the island—and later in the evening there was dancing. We Australians, however, did not dance. We were awkward from being so long out of practice, and we were, also, so much too tall for the local girls, literally towering above them.

We began at once to organise the regiment on proper military lines. We chose the market area for our training ground for all foot work, and I managed to obtain several American drill books from Lieutenant Bagis, who was the Quartermaster. These had to be studied carefully, for there were many differences between the American methods of instruction and words of command and our own. However, with the help of the typewriter, I soon produced a syllabus of training, while Jim collected many stores and, with the aid of a few tools and a party of men, erected rifle rests and targets.

The necessary equipment for a Signal Class was also got together. I got this by appealing to householders for any pieces of white cloth which could be spared. I then organised a working-party of women to sew hems on them wide enough to take sticks or poles. I took school every morning, and during the afternoons and evenings I concentrated upon teaching signallers the Morse Code.

Everybody else was also busy. Captain Steele took over the island administration. He often worked all day until after dark. Rex Blow and Miles Gillon usually spent the mornings taking parties of soldiers into the jungle, to blaze new trails and to set up food supply huts for future use. In the afternoons they took the classes in school. Jock and Jim helped me, and Rex Butler was made " Finance Minister." He had a full-time job, for besides collecting the allowances and paying the accounts, he was responsible for obtaining food and supervising the cooking.

About four miles west from our quarters there was a high and solitary mountain, known to us as Thumb Hill. I suggested one day to Charlie, that if it were possible to reach the summit of this mountain without too great exertion, it might be possible to establish a signal unit there, which would be of great value, for from it we should be able to spot approaching planes and enemy shipping, and so be able to give warning of coming trouble. Charlie thought it was an excellent idea, and taking Jim with him, he set off to investigate the possibilities. The report when he returned was most encouraging. From the mountain top it was possible to observe all the surrounding country and the water-ways, and a track was laid by which, with the help of some native-made ladders, the summit could be reached by a signal party, as soon as the men were sufficiently trained to send signals.

One of our early troubles was that there were no clocks available, and we found that, to the Philippino soldiers " near enough " was good enough. But it was not good enough for us. We wanted parades and we wanted them punctually, and I had to set about finding some method of letting everyone know the time. I erected a sun stick in an open place, and the shadow was measured at midday. Ray, who had a watch, was made time-keeper, and a large gong was obtained, which was sounded at stated times. This helped considerably in mustering the troops, and we were able to get them on parade punctually.

Colonel Suarez came frequently to visit our school, and

was greatly impressed by the standards we had attained. He sent recommendations to the Australian Army H.Q., with which he was in touch, requesting that I should be promoted to be Warrant Officer, and Jim, Jock and Rex Butler, to be sergeants. These Field Promotions meant a lot to us, not only in our pay, but to our prestige. The reports sent by the Colonel were extremely gratifying. Mine read :

" To be Warrant Officer—Sgt. Walter Wallace, NX 58809, Chief Recruit Instructor. Our troops are greatly indebted to this man for the excellent instruction given, whereas he spends practically 24 hours a day to improve the men in command, for any eventualities. I consider Sgt. Major Wallace the best instructor I have had."
(Signed) Alejandro Suarez, P.C., Lieut.-Col. C.O.

The reports on Butler, Kennedy, and McLaren were equally commendatory.

Our first examinations were held on the seventeenth of July, and the results were more than satisfactory, and we all felt encouraged to continue with the instruction. That day was an exciting one altogether, for during the afternoon a report was received from a fisherman that some survivors from a torpedoed Japanese ship had been washed ashore on the neighbouring island of Manuk Manko, which was just a few miles to the south of Tawi Tawi. This news caused a great stir, and our two Rex's were sent off in a kompit with a patrol of soldiers to investigate and, if possible, to bring back prisoners. While they were away, there was more excitement. Two distinguished visitors arrived at our station, in the persons of Captain J. A. Hamner, and Lieutenant Kane, from a submarine. They were American radio operators, who had been sent to Tawi Tawi in the hope of being able to transmit useful information from the island to the South-West Pacific Area. Their gear was brought up from the jetty to our place, which we had christened Anzac House, and there was great jubilation among us when from it we were handed out American cigarettes, Australia Log Cabin tobacco, and Tally-Ho papers. We were also presented with biscuits, chocolates, and articles of clothing. We had a regular gala night of it that night!

Our visitors had with them a pedal radio, which they intended to set up in the jungle near by. This was going to make my signalling plan really effective, and I stepped up my training and had my crew working as they had never worked before.

The next morning the party we had sent to Manuk Manko returned, bringing with them a large batch of Japanese who were now *our* prisoners. The local population went mad with excitement. They rushed up and down the roadway as the Japs were marched along, shouting angry words and waving their krisses and parangs in a threatening manner. The position of us Australians was rather critical, for we had to make a shield between our prisoners and the native people who were out for blood. As I assisted in herding the Japanese into a large bamboo stockade, I thought of the floggings and tortures and starvation diet we had undergone in Sandakan and reflected how ironically the position was now changed.

Captain Hamner soon had his radio in operation and made contact with Australia, and with the Guerilla H.Q. at Butuan, which was somewhere north-east of our present position. We received war news from all parts of the globe, and it was strange to hear again a voice say : " This is Australia."

But although the training was going so well, we had plenty of troubles. For one thing, malaria was prevalent on the island, and many of us went down with severe bouts of fever which interrupted the work considerably. Another worry was that we quickly discovered that we had traitors among us in the shape of fifth columnists. We were warned to be on the alert, and we had to watch all our native soldiers very carefully, for we did not know which of them we could trust.

It was on July the twenty-second that I first visited Thumb Hill. The climb was the hardest day's work I had done for a long time, and I was glad to sit down and rest when at last I and my party reached the top. When we had recovered a little, we moved over to the east side of the mountain from which a view of Batu Batu could be obtained. Jim had already fixed up a platform in a tall tree, on which a look-out could sit and see without being seen, being completely con-

cealed by leaves and branches. My job now was to place a
series of such look-out posts, so that observations could be
made in all directions. A flat, jungle-type table was fashioned,
on which I fixed a piece of cardboard. On this I drew a circle,
dividing the circle into 360 degrees. With the aid of a compass I fastened the circle so that zero was pointing due north.
When this had been done, a nail was hammered exactly in the
centre. A piece of string was tied to the nail, with a pin at the
other end of it, and with this set-up we were in a position to
take a bearing to any ship that might appear off the coast. Jim
was fixing up the same kind of arrangement on the Batu Batu
side of the summit. We could now take accurate observations
of shipping on both sides of the island, and with the help of
signals we could let those below know exactly where any vessel
might be.

The signallers were now as perfect as we could hope to get
them in the circumstances. They could both send and receive
messages in detail, and it was with pride and pleasure and
elation that I opened communications between Thumb Hill
and Batu Batu. The men themselves were delighted. They felt
themselves to be the eyes of Tawi Tawi, not only able to
communicate with the other islands in sight, but also able to
tell their fellow islands in Tawi Tawi all that was happening
around their coasts. The hill made a splendid observation post.
On the north we overlooked the Sulu Sea, and a large part of
the Sulu archipelago, and in the far north-west we could sight
the part of Borneo known as Tambisan Point. The Celebes Sea
was on the west, in the sonth-west was the Sibutu Passage and
the island of Bongao. In the south was Siminal and numerous
other islands. With this wide range of ocean before us, it was
obvious that we might be able to transmit much useful information to the station at Batu Batu.

It was not long before we had a chance to prove our efficiency. A boat appeared out of the north-east, moving along
the northern coast of Tawi Tawi in a southerly direction. At
once her details were noted, her range, speed, weight, and size,
calculated, and her type of armament observed. The man on
duty flagged VE. VE. VE. VE. (I want to speak to you). Batu
Batu answered, and the full message was sent:

ENEMY SHIP APPR. FROM NE TO SW, RANGE 7000. SPEED
11. WEIGHT 3000. ARM 4-IN. ON BOW. BRIDGE CENTRE.
TWO MASTS. BEARING 48. ACK.

Our first message was away! It told the station down at
Batu Batu that an enemy ship was approaching from the
north-east and heading towards the south-west, and that its
distance from our observation point was estimated at about
7000 yards. The vessel with its speed, weight, and armament,
was described, and the message finished by asking the other
station to acknowledge. In addition, the message was relayed
to Captain Hamner down below, so that it could be trans-
mitted by radio to South-West Pacific Area for their necessary
action.

In this way, we should often, we hoped, be able to summon
Allied submarines to sink enemy shipping, and I felt a grim
satisfaction, knowing that the station was going to be successful and that I should be able to avenge my murdered comrades through my work.

The signal station also served to warn us when enemy planes
were approaching. A flag waving in a circle was the sign of
this. One day a Japanese plane came over and circled several
times over Thumb Hill, and over our H.Q. below. The pilot
was obviously searching out targets for future bombing, and
from the way he flew over the vulnerable spots, we felt sure
that our positions had been previously made known to him,
and that we had fifth columnists in our midst. It was an unpleasant thought and we kept an even more careful watch
upon our men. Whoever the traitor was, he was smart and
intelligent, and we could only hope that he would one day
make a false move which would give him away and enable us
to foil the treachery.

I had a very narrow escape from death one day when I
was climbing up to Thumb Hill for an inspection tour. I had
almost reached the top of the jungle ladder which helped us
up the last, steepest mountain face, when looking up, I saw,
curled around an overhanging branch just above my head, a
deadly snake. I nearly fainted on the spot, but pulling myself
together, I continued my climb and got safely to the top and

then prepared to make an end of the dangerous creature. One of my men called out to me:

"Sir, don't shoot it! It is the guardian of the mountain. Anyone who kills it will die in three days!"

I looked at the man, and I looked at the snake. And then I said:

"If that creature attacks you or anyone else, you or he would be dead in three minutes!" And I shot it. For the next three days all eyes looked at me in awed anticipation wherever I went, and I must admit I was slightly uneasy about it myself. But the crisis passed, and I was still alive, and after that I was gazed upon with reverence as well as with awe. I think the men thought I must be under some special divine protection to have survived.

CHAPTER VII

THE JAPANESE CLOSE IN

DURING MY watches on Thumb Hill, I noticed that there was another isolated mountain on the island of Bongao, and it occurred to me that if this other mountain could be climbed, we might set up another observation post on it, and so considerably lengthen our lines of communication. I told Ray of my idea, and we decided to investigate, and to take Captain Hamner with us. So in the early hours of August the first, we all three set sail in a small vinta—a native sail boat with outriggers—for the island.

With a favourable wind, it did not take us long to arrive at our destination. A guide was made available to us from the local battalion, and we set off through the jungle towards the mountain. But we had not gone far when we realised that we could never get there. The jungle was so dense that it was almost pitch black within it, and the air was stifling. We ran into a tropical storm, and, to add to our troubles, I lost the heels off both my boots which made walking very difficult.

After several hours of struggling in the jungle, we decided to return home. But when we came within sight of the shore, we saw, steaming towards the island, a large steam launch full of Japs. The only arms in our possession were a pistol apiece—no match for an armed patrol vessel. So we stayed under cover on the verge of the jungle and watched while the launch pulled into the wharf. Unaware that they were being watched, the Japanese disembarked and proceeded to a near-by pool for a bath. If only we had had tommy guns with us what a surprise we could have given them! As it was it was hopeless to try to attack them, and after a hurried conference we decided to make for Tawi Tawi, and return after darkness with a stronger force.

We could not get to the spot where we had beached the vinta we came in, but a little farther along the shore we found another and set off for home. It was late in the night when we arrived at our H.Q. and we were told when we reached it that our signallers had observed the Japanese launch and the landing, and an ambush patrol had been sent to Bangao —Rex, Miles, Jim, and Jock, and a party of Philippino soldiers. We three were very sorry we had missed them and lost the chance of joining in the fun, and we decided that the least we could do now was to sit up until they came back. But about dawn sleep got the better of us, and we had just dozed off when we were awakened again by the droning of plane engines overhead, and the next moment a bomb came screeching down.

Our house vibrated from the force of the explosion, and we were all out like a shot, jumping the front veranda rails and bolting across the road to fall flat on our faces just as another bomb descended. This one did not do much harm, but just as the plane came circling in for another shot, two young Philippino soldiers suddenly jumped up and ran to rescue the two flags which were flying from the barrack flag poles. The third bomb got them, and the two brave lads fell, clutching the flags they had tried so heroically to save.

Six bombs in all were dropped, after which there were several bursts of machine-gun fire before the plane finally took its departure. It had not really done much damage to property, though how it had managed to miss the barracks and our house we could not imagine. It was broad daylight, the two targets stood out plainly, and there had been absolutely no opposition. The pilot had been able to come down as low as he liked. Yet neither had been hit.

During the afternoon two more soldiers died from wounds, and the four funerals were conducted with full military honours. One of the victims was a Morro, and in his case the service was carried out in accordance with his tribe's religious customs, with much weeping and singing, his body being lowered into the grave wrapped in the flag for which he had died. It was an impressive ceremony, and after all four burials were completed, we returned to our quarters, sad at heart to think that we had lost four of our best men.

Rex Butler was told to find another house for our H.Q., and this time to be sure that it was not near the barracks. He found a convenient one and we moved into it at once. But we knew that it would not be any safer than the old one for long. Our fifth columnists would be sure to let the Japs know where it was in time.

The raiding party returned that evening, full of excitement over their venture. They reported that they had landed under cover of darkness, and had crept forward through the jungle till they reached the rear of the wharf where the launch was lying. Positions were taken up, and when, about six o'clock, the patrol ship began to move away, a barrage of fire was opened up on her. Her captain came up on the bridge holding a pair of binoculars. He offered an easy target and in a moment he had crash-dived down to the deck below. Two officers were then picked off, and several members of the crew who were on deck. A massed fire was then concentrated on the rudder, but though taking an erratic course, the ship moved on its way.

None of our men was hurt, and we shared the jubilation they all exhibited, although we realised that sooner or later there would be reprisals, and we should have to pay for the audacious attempt to sink or capture the patrol boat. The reprisals duly came. A few weeks later, the Hill Station reported that a two-thousand-ton vessel was approaching Batu Batu from the south. Most of the people at once made off into the bush. Even the soldiers disappeared, and our guard, who was on duty at the wharf, instead of sounding the warning gong with which he had been provided, flung it into the sea and rushed into the jungle.

Rex Blow immediately went to a secret rendezvous to try to muster the troops. Jim and Ray and I collected the few men we could find and followed him along the secret jungle trails. We were all worried, for we knew that the approaching boat could carry from two to three thousand men, so that it would be possible for several different landings to be made, not only at Batu Batu, but at other places as well. However, there was nothing that we could do but try to get the troops together again, and we pushed off into the jungle to try to ferret out our disappearing soldiers.

We gathered up a certain number of them, and, since it was now quite dark, we bivouacked for the night. In the morning, to our disgust, we found that half the troops we had mustered had disappeared. They had gone bush again. This time it seemed useless to try to retrieve them, so Ray and Jim and I, together with the few men who had stayed with us, pushed on to our rendezvous. After crossing a river, we joined forces once more with Captain Hamner, Lieutenant Kane, and Miles Gillon. Charlie and Jock, we learned, were out together, trying to gather information.

During that day, two Japanese planes came over. They each dropped six bombs, then methodically machine-gunned the whole area. We crouched flat on the ground while the bombs exploded and during the gunning which followed. It seemed ages before it was over and the planes had disappeared. They had not killed any of us this time, but it had been a nasty experience. When it was all over, I said to Ray :
" It's very suspicious. When we are in the village the village is bombed. When we are in the jungle, the jungle is bombed."

Ray agreed that it was strangely suspicious, and we both came to the conclusion that our various positions and hide-outs must have been carefully charted, and the chart sent by some traitor to the Japanese on Jolo. We felt that this particular traitor knew too much to be merely an ordinary soldier, and that we would have to look for him among the officers and the N.C.O.s, and not among the men.

Since so much was known to the enemy, we were now compelled to choose other positions and to re-organise. Jim helped Captain Hamner to find another place in which to set up his radio, Ray and I rounded up stragglers, while Miles and Rex Blow drifted back to Batu Batu to try to locate Charlie and Jock. Rex Butler was kept busy supervising supplies. Our signallers on Thumb Hill and down at the Home Station had behaved well, and had been active ever since the first warning of the enemy ship had been given.

The food position was far from satisfactory, so it was decided that I should help Rex, and scout around to try to find further supplies. A Morro Lieutenant was allotted to me as a guide and interpreter and we set off. During our travels over the next few days, I noticed that he disappeared from time to time for a little while, and each time that he did so it was always in the same direction. I grew suspicious, and being now a past master at the tracking game, I decided to trail him secretly. The next time he made off I followed and observed him slip a piece of paper under the closed door of a jungle shack.

He had had no idea that I had followed him, and I played dumb and did not let him see that I had any doubts about him. Later, though, I told Charlie. He investigated the matter, with the result that this officer was arrested, tried, found guilty, and duly executed. In war, there is no room for sentiment in cases such as this. It is a matter of kill or be killed. The following day, the Hill Signal Station reported that two native boats had gone out to a large Japanese ship which had slowed down when passing the island, and that a bag had been handed up to the ship. On their return the owners of the small boats were arrested, found guilty of supplying information to the enemy, and beheaded.

On August the tenth, we had a welcome addition to our forces in the shape of four Americans who had been prisoners on Palawan Island and had managed to escape. They were Lieutenant Davis, Private Sid Wright, a Marine, Bruce Elliott, from the Navy, and a man called Bob. They all joined Captain Hamner's force.

During this period, our signallers had all remained loyal. They were jubilant, too, I discovered, when I next found time to visit them. Many explosions had been heard in and around the Celebes Seas, indicating that enemy ships had probably been sunk. They felt proud and happy to think that the information they had passed down to Batu Batu, which had then been radioed by Captain Hamner to the South-West Pacific Area, had been instrumental in bringing about the sinking of some of these vessels. The whole job, in fact, was good for their morale, for they were conscious that theirs was a position of trust, and that they were responsible for warning, not only the forces, but also their friends and relations among the civil population, of approaching danger.

I spent a good deal of my time up on Thumb Hill, and in between spottings, I taught them some Australian songs, *Nursie, Anzac,* and an old favourite of mine, *Leave Me With A Smile.* They loved playing cards, but I was a bit too much of a professional at card games, and I won so often that I was debarred from playing at last. One day, when I was feeling rather bored, a corporal came over to me and said :

" Sir, would you like to learn to speak our language?"

" Sure, I would," I said, for I thought it might be useful to address my men direct, in their own tongue, instead of having to rely upon an interpreter, and we started off on a lesson there and then. I asked him to tell me what to say if I wanted to call a man to come to me.

" Currie-co," he told me.

I memorised this, and then said :

" And if I want to call all the men?"

" Currie-co-mo," he replied.

The next morning I tried out my new-found knowledge.

" Currie-co-mo!" I called.

Not a man moved, so I called again. Still no one made the slightest effort to obey the order. I called the corporal over and asked him why.

" Oh, sir," he said. " All these men come from different islands from the one I come from, and each island has its own dialect so that they do not understand what you said."

There are about a thousand islands in the Philippine group, so it seemed that the two words I had might be said in a thousand different ways.

" But how on earth do you get on if you visit another island and you want to talk to someone?" I inquired.

" Oh, sir, that is easy," he told me. " I just find someone who can speak English."

After that there didn't seem much point in going on with the language lessons.

We had been warned that a certain tribe of Morros known as " The Black Teeth," were helping the Japanese in their raids. They showed them the jungle trails, and often joined in the murdering and plundering and raping that the Japs carried out. We discovered that a party of these men were hiding in the jungle, and an attack was arranged to drive them out of Tawi Tawi. Miles, Rex Blow, Jock, and Rex Butler, headed the contingent sent to carry out the job. The rest of us, reluctantly, had to remain behind and await results. I was worried about the whole thing from the beginning, for I felt that our folks were not in sufficient strength to go into an area about which they knew next to nothing to wage war on people who knew every inch of the territory. It would have been a dangerous expedition anyway, and as it happened it was made even more so by the fact that we had amongst us, though we did not know it then, a man who had relatives fighting for the enemy. He managed to send them information about our proposed attack, and our force was ambushed on the way. The men put up a gallant resistance, but the odds against them were too heavy, and they were obliged at last to withdraw—with the loss of our pal, Rex Butler, who was killed in the skirmish. Miles was wounded too, but fortunately Rex Blow managed to get to him and dragged him back to safety.

The only consolation for this tragic affair was that several of the Black Teeth had been killed, among them the traitor.

Malaria now attacked us, not surprisingly in view of the numbers of mosquitoes. I had a nasty turn of it, and so did most of the others. Many of the civilian population died, owing to the lack of medical supplies. Each time a death occurred, the victim's family and friends held a ceremony known as " Last Prayers." It went on for nine days and nine nights, during which there was dancing, and singing, as well as prayers and fasting. It was puzzling to our ideas to see how gay and bright these mourning occasions always were.

During August, we Aussies held a conference to discuss how best we could show our appreciation to the many people who had shown us kindness since we came to Tawi Tawi. We decided to give a party, a dinner, followed by singing, and we sent invitations to thirty families, asking one member from each. Our place was not over-large and we thought that thirty guests were about as many as we could manage. The big night arrived, and everything looked splendid. The decorations were really beautiful and the cook had prepared a first-class meal. Punctually at seven-thirty the guests began to arrive. Jock went to the door and then uttered an exclamation of horror. And no wonder! Instead of thirty visitors, we found that we had over a hundred—and more could be seen coming along. Each of our thirty householders had not only brought along his whole family, but a number of his friends as well—and we had only provided food for thirty, with just a bit over for the staff.

We were in a flat spin. But somehow we managed. None of us got a mouthful of food ourselves, but we succeeded in giving each of our guests something, and the evening turned out to be quite a success after all. We Aussies sang Australian songs, and, in return, some of our girl visitors danced for us their native dances.

Our neighbouring islands, we learned, were now being systematically bombed and raided by the Japanese, aided by their Black Teeth allies. They murdered, and looted, and burnt the houses down wherever they landed. Why the Japs had to behave so barbarously was a puzzle to me. They expected the people to co-operate with them—yet they had to treat them in this devilish way! Large numbers of the natives were now leaving their own islands and coming to Tawi Tawi for protection. Kompits and vintas, laden with refugees and their belongings, landed on our coast every day. We were also getting regular visits from Japanese observation planes, and Japanese ships passed more frequently. We felt that we were probably due for our turn of bombing and raiding very shortly.

Then Colonel Suarez arrived at our H.Q. and told us that arrangements were being made to move us Australians and the Americans to General Headquarters, which were in another part of the Philippines " somewhere north." Our feelings at hearing this news were rather mixed. We were glad to be moving on for some things, but we had been very happy living with these lovable people, and it was going to be hard to say goodbye to them, and to the men whom we had trained.

Knowing that the order to move might come at any time, we held a conference to decide whether we should go in relays or all at one time. It could not exactly be called a round table conference, for Charlie and Jock were lying on the floor, laid low by malaria, and Jim and I, though now nearly over our turns of it, were still sick men. After some discussion we made up our minds to stick together, for though we were all suffering from malaria more or less, we seemed to go down by relays, not all at once. If we stayed together, the chances were that some of us would be well enough to help those who were laid out, so we made up our minds not to separate when the time came.

A day or two later we got a message over the radio from Divisional H.Q. in Butuan, that all the personnel of the A.I.F. on the island of Tawi Tawi were to report to General H.Q. in north-east Agusan a state many miles north-east from where we were. We were told that the journey would be very dangerous, as we should have to proceed by kompit up the west coast of Mindanao Province, running the gauntlet through Japanese-held sea. We were reassured, however, that with " great care " we could make it.

Our life on Tawi Tawi was now coming to an end, but we had to undergo some more bombing and a raid from the Japs before we left the island. We also received a message from the enemy, directed especially to us Australians. A plane flew overhead and dropped a paper demanding our surrender, and telling us to go to a certain point where we should be met, " bringing our shovels with us." To dig our own graves presumably! Needless to say, it was a message we did not reply to.

It was on the twenty-second of October that we had our worst day of bombing. The planes came over first about eight-thirty in the morning, dropping twelve bombs and doing a little cannon practice before they flew away. Later in the day another plane came, dropped more bombs and raked the area where we were with cannon fire. When the all-clear sounded, an inspection was made of the damage, but, apart from a number of pot-holes, there was none. Not a thing had been hit.

Two days later, we were awakened about five o'clock by the noise of running feet, and jumping out of bed we saw our soldiers rushing along the roadway. They had news for us— a big ship was anchored off the beach at Batu Batu. Rex, Charlie, Jock, and I, moved up to a small hill, well covered with bush, from which we could get a clear view of the southern water. Sure enough, the boat was there—a three-thousand-ton cargo vessel which could carry anything up to two thousand troops.

We rushed back to our quarters and set things in motion. A runner was sent to warn Captain Hamner so that he could dismantle his radio and go to earth. Ray, and one of the men, went off with the records to a secret hideout, and the rest of us picked up our gear and made off up the roadway. I turned aside to have another look at the signallers on the Hill as we went, and flagged a message telling them to pull up the ladder and sit tight, and wishing them good luck.

Five small boats were now lowered from the mother ship, all loaded with troops. They headed for the beach. Two armed motor boats and an armed tug were firing machine guns, giving protective cover, and we had only gone a little way along the road when the large vessel opened up and began firing shells in our direction. After a bit, we found that they were working to a certain pattern. A shell was dropped at a given range, the next would fall so much ahead a little to the right, the third still farther ahead on the other flank. As soon as we had grasped the method, we were able to move forward fairly safely, though we had to be careful, just in case a shell fell short. As usual, nothing was hit, apart from a tree here and there. Had the Japs used shrapnel shells, fitted with time fuses set to burst in the air, they might have caught someone, but, as it was, they did nothing except make a noise and a few small holes in the jungle.

When I and my signallers from the home station caught up with Rex and Jim, we tried to find some of the troops so that we could set an ambush for the invaders. But not a man could we find anywhere; all our soldiers, apart from the few we had with us, had vanished into the jungle. Behind us the Japanese and the Black Teeth had landed and were now engaged in burning down the houses in Batu Batu. From a rise, we could see black smoke rising from our own home, Anzac House. It was galling to watch all those houses go up in smoke. Where were the troops? Why hadn't they stayed with us? If only they had there would have been more than enough of us to wipe out that raiding party. Everything was in our favour if only the soldiers had stood firm, the lie of the land, the wonderful cover, knowledge of the country. But as it was we could do nothing, and we decided to plunge into the jungle and see if we could pick up a few more men there.

We roped in a few as we pushed on, and presently came out upon the roadway again. We saw several houses blazing in the distance, among them Captain Hamner's. Not far from where we were, there was a house, at present untouched, in which we saw someone moving about. Knowing that all civilians had been evacuated, we wondered who it could be, and decided to investigate. Creeping up we surrounded the house on all sides, and were about to open fire when someone saw that it was a woman inside. We caught her and questioned her, and discovered that she had been sent back by her husband, who was a soldier hiding in the jungle, to fetch some article he had forgotten. He had told her that if she was caught by the Japanese she was to say that she knew nothing about anything. *Had* it been the Japs who caught her instead of us, she would certainly have said nothing!

We walked along the roadway, going very carefully, and feeling pretty sore about the behaviour of the men we had trained, when we came upon two soldiers who told us that the enemy had now left the island. Lying by the side of the road was another man, dead. The two survivors told us that the three of them had set off on their own to do what they could. They had set up their own little ambush, and had succeeded in killing one of the Japs. Then the enemy had captured one of them. I went over to look at him, I saw that his head had been cut off, and a large piece of flesh sliced from his thigh. Sickened by the sight, I went after the others, but though I felt grieved at the loss of this brave man, I was comforted to think that our training had not been altogether wasted. Some of our men a least knew their duty and did it, regardless of consequences.

I went off into the jungle soon after this episode, to one of our secret food stores to arrange for supplies to be sent back to Batu Batu, since I knew that the enemy would have left little behind. When I reached it, there to my amazement were some forty odd soldiers, all calmly sleeping. I went quite mad with rage at the sight of them, and told them just what I thought of them. I told them that their homes had all been burned down, but if only they had done their duty and stayed with us, we could have destroyed the enemy and saved their houses and belongings.

Some of the men pleaded that they had malaria, but I told them that that excuse would not have washed with the Japs, and that, anyway, the speed with which they got to their feet when I came upon them showed that they were not very ill. I made them chop up a large pile of wood and get a roaring fire going so that we could cook a meal. After we had fed, I made them load up with supplies and come back with me to Batu Batu. They had all forgotten their malaria by this time.

Batu Batu, we found, had been practically razed to the ground. Of course all the houses in these islands burnt very easily, and could be quickly rebuilt, but the people's possessions could not so easily be replaced. It seemed an outrageous thing to do, to bring such destruction to a simple, primitive people. Later in the day some of the women came back to the village in the hope of saving some of their belongings, but there was nothing left. It was pitiful to watch them moving about their ruined homes, tears blinding them as they searched in vain for some cherished article.

That night Charlie and I went down to the jetty, for we had a job to do. It was very dark, perfect for our purpose. The Japanese had left several buoys behind, marking the deep water for future occasions. We intended to move them. Taking a kompit and a few soldiers we moved cautiously out to a buoy which we towed gently to shallow water. We did the same thing to all the buoys in turn. We did not remove them altogether, for that would have aroused suspicion. But by bringing them to shallow water, we hoped that some, at least, of future raiding boats might founder.

We got back safely, and soon after the Colonel arrived, bringing with him the four Americans. He had come to tell us the final arrangements for our leaving Tawi Tawi. Now that it had come to the point, we were all very sorry to be going, and told the Colonel so. The Colonel, who was a lovable old man, seemed as sorry to say goodbye to us as we were at saying it to him. He told us how much he appreciated all that we had done, and before he left he called me aside, and holding both my hands tight, he said:

"Thanks, Wallace, for a really magnificent job! We are deeply indebted to you." He nearly cried as he said it.

I nearly cried, too, as he turned away. I had grown very fond of him, and of all these people. They had taken us into their homes, and saved us, and fed us, and we felt that we owed them a debt which we could never repay. And apart from all that they had done for us, they were a delightful people to know. Their laws and customs were a source of unending interest to me. Their moral code is stern, and there is no such thing as living in adultery. If persons are found guilty of such a crime, they are immediately executed. Execution, too, is the punishment for a crime known as "Touching a Female"—that is, no man is allowed to touch a female, not even on the arm or the shoulder to attract her attention, unless he is her husband, father, or brother. If he does and is detected, the penalty is death.

Yet if a man marries a woman and she has not given him a child within two years of his marriage, he is allowed to call in his father, brothers, and if necessary even his half-brothers, to help him to produce a child. He usually has plenty of half-brothers, too, for another custom of the country is that if a mother is unable to feed her baby herself and a wet-nurse is called in, the two babies feeding from the same breast become half-brothers—or half-sisters, as the case may be. Until this was explained to us we had often wondered why there were so many half-brothers and sisters in the place. With all these males to draw upon as substitutes, if a man could not get an heir it was just too bad.

CHAPTER VIII

THROUGH ENEMY SEAS

I T H A D been arranged that we were to walk to Tarawakan, where we were to embark for our voyage. We went in relays, and Ray, Rex, Jim, and I, left Batu Batu about five-thirty the next day. Charlie and Jock were to follow a little later, and we were to meet Captain Hamner and the Americans on the coast. We were all loaded up with gear, and we went along the road which we had traversed on our arrival in Tawi Tawi. Once more the people lined up to see us pass, but this time instead of cheering, they seemed absolutely heart-broken to see us go. Many sad farewells were said as we marched along.

About halfway to our destination, I was obliged to stop, as a sudden attack of malaria came on. After consultation, it was decided that I should wait by the roadside until Charlie and Jock came along, which would give me a chance to feel a bit better. A native brought me some hot coffee and a couple of tablets, and I lay down, shivering and sweating, to give the stuff time to work. While I lay there, Captain Hamner and the Americans passed by, carrying a terrific load, most of which consisted of radio and supply stores. I was still feeling very bad when Charlie and Jock came along, about two in the morning. They were surprised and concerned at my condition, but I had to move on now, somehow, so they helped me to my feet and got me at length to Tarawakan. I was all in by the time we got there, and I just dropped down on the ground and fell asleep. When I awoke, some hours later, I found that the others had covered me up with all the spare clothes available, and though I was still shivering, the worst of the attack seemed to have passed.

It had been arranged for two kompits to take us away from Tawi Tawi, one for us Australians, with Bruce and Sid and two native boys, the other for Captain Hamner and his party and four natives. Captain Hamner's boat arrived first, but it was found that some slight repair work was needed on it, so it was taken away to be overhauled, with instructions that it was to be kept under cover until dark. Our kompit then arrived. It was loaded with our gear, and then, like the other taken into hiding until night. During the day the sun came out, and finished off my fever, and soon I was on my feet again. In the afternoon, Colonel Suarez came once more to see how things were going and again we had to go through the painful business of saying goodbye. His Quartermaster, Lieutenant Bagis, was with him, and he presented me, as a memento, with the kriss—the wavy, double-edged sword of the east—which had belonged to the officer whom I had caught doing fifth column work.

Darkness fell, and at nine o'clock our kompit glided into shore, quietly and smoothly, leaving scarcely a ripple on the water in its rear. We climbed in and were pushed off, and soon we were heading for a small, uninhabited island off the coast, where we were to rest for the night, and organise ourselves for the long trip that lay ahead. Charlie was once more in charge of the expedition, for now we had been struck " Off Strength " of the 125th Infantry Regiment and were again escaped Australian soldiers, running the gauntlet through the Japanese-held Philippine seas.

The thirtieth of October, 1943, found us, then, on a small, desolate island, inhabited chiefly by mosquitoes. For the early part of the day, the wind blew from the north, which, since it was north we had to go, was of no help to us. During the afternoon, however, it swung round, and it was decided that we should push off as soon as darkness fell. We had to pass close by the strongly-guarded island of Jolo, and it was felt that it would be safer to do this during the night. Rex and Jock spent the waiting time fashioning cups and plates of sorts out of coconuts, and Charlie and Jim went down to have a good look at the boat by daylight. It was fortunate that they did, for they discovered that it had developed a serious leak. Jim tried to repair the damage, but found that it was quite beyond him, so, instead of setting out on our northward voyage as we had intended, we had to turn back and make for Tarawakan again. We had to bail out all the way, and it would have been almost certain death had we attempted to go forward in such a condition.

We made the shore in a sheltered spot, about half a mile from Tarawakan. Here we unloaded our gear, and the rest of us stayed under cover, while Charlie and Ray took the kompit off to try and exchange it for another. Ray returned on November the first, about eleven at night, with a brand new kompit which had only just come off the slips. Charlie had stayed behind to fix up the financial details. He turned up in the morning, and by seven o'clock we had loaded up, and were at last on our northward way. We stopped a little farther up the coast to lay in a supply of bananas and coconuts and fresh water, and at nine o'clock we finally left Tawi Tawi.

There was little wind, so the crew pulled out the oars and began to row. Except for me, we all took turns with them, but I had a double hernia so was told not to attempt any rowing, for there would have been no possibility of getting any medical aid if things went wrong. Instead I was given the job of Look-Out Man, and it kept me fully occupied, for there were all kinds of craft moving about. We had not been going long when I saw eight kompits heading towards us. This caused us some consternation, and we Aussies all lay low, stretched out on the floor of the kompit with our rifles at the ready for use if necessary. The two natives rowed bravely on. Our position was perilous, for we were between two pro-Japanese islands, and Jolo was only a short distance away. However, the eight kompits passed by without taking any notice of us, and after a bit we came up, feeling very relieved.

We rowed all that day, picking our way through the maze of small islands until we found a suitable resting place for the night. It was a tiny sandy islet, all on its own, and we chose it because, being entirely destitute of cover, apart from two small bushes, we were able to make sure before landing that no enemies were there. That is, no enemies except for mosquitoes. They were there in their thousands—and what they lived on before we turned up, we couldn't imagine. They allowed us very little sleep that night. In the morning there was no wind at all, so we had to stay put all that day, and the best part of the next one, too, with nothing to do but cut our hair, play cards, and explore the island. Exploring the island took Charlie and me exactly ten minutes, for it was really nothing more than a sand bank sticking out of the sea. We found two turtle eggs, though, which was something.

Late in the afternoon of our second day on the sand bank, a wind suddenly sprang up, and we clambered on board as quickly as possible and pushed off. The wind developed gale force, and our kompit began to move at last. The gale soon got violent, and before we knew what was happening, our sail split from top to bottom. It was a miracle that we did not turn turtle there and then. Somehow the crew managed to haul down what was left of the sail, and got to work trying to repair the damage. It was useless to try to steer or row. All we could do was to cling on as best we could to some of the boat, while the waves tossed us up and down. One moment we would be high on the crest of a wave, the next deep down in a trough with the water towering above us. To make matters worse, we were all violently seasick, as we were pitched from side to side of our boat.

How we ever survived that storm, I don't know. It went on all that night, and in the morning it was still blowing hard. We had got the sail up, but it soon split again. However, we sewed it together once more and got it up, and then, as suddenly as it had begun, the wind stopped blowing and the sea began to calm down. But we had been blown right off our course, and instead of sailing along the west coast of Basilan as we had intended, we found that we were nearing the islands of East and West Bolod, many miles east of our objective.

We were now in a pretty pickle. The wind had dropped completely, and we were becalmed in a still sea with Japanese-held islands all around us. We were, too, all as sick and miserable as we could well be. However, we had to pull ourselves together and do what we could, so out came the oars again, and all hands set to work to row towards East Bolod, the nearest land we could make.

We reached the island, hungry and thirsty and worn out with fatigue, and very uncertain as to what kind of a reception we should meet with. One of our natives recognised the people about on the little jetty as Plows, a race that lives on its vintas and exists by fishing. We sent him to talk to them and gather what news he could, and after a bit he came back and told us that the Japanese were in the habit of visiting the island every two days of so, but they had been the day before and there were none there now. So, since we were all so done in, we decided to spend the night there. However, we took the precaution of sleeping in relays, and we kept a sharp watch in case any of the craft pushed off to carry information to our enemy. But the precautions were not necessary. The people did not seem to bother about us one way or the other. We would have liked to stay for a couple of days to recover from our experiences, but in view of what the natives had told our boy about the Japs' visiting habits, we felt that it would be too dangerous. So the next morning we put off, and set our course for an island called Pilas Island which we could just see in the distance. We knew that this island was inhabited and that there was plenty of vegetation, and we intended to have a good rest when we got there, and stay perhaps for a couple of days.

But when we reached it, after hours of hard rowing in the blazing sun, the people begged us not to stop. The Japanese visited them frequently, and they were terrified lest harbouring us should get them into trouble. So we stayed only long enough to replenish our water supply and collect a few coconuts, and then we moved off-shore, and lay-to, waiting for a favourable wind to come up. The next stage of our journey was one of the most dangerous. We had to cross the Basilan Straits, situated between Basilan Island and the State of Mindanao on the mainland. Japanese ships used the straits constantly, and it would be necessary to be able to move quickly when we ventured into this perilous waterway.

About five o'clock on the morning of November the seventh, the breeze appeared to be favourable, so we got under way. Luck was with us. The wind soon became stronger and was just where we wanted it to be. Our large, square sail billowed out, and we sailed on comfortably right through the day until, about a quarter to five in the evening, a patrol boat was observed off our starboard bow.

We knew that the cursed thing would carry machine guns, and possibly a radio, and we thought that the game was up. However, we lay doggo once more, our rifles at the ready, determined to make a fight for it, anyway. We would let the patrol boat come right alongside. Then, from our allocated positions, we would pick off the gunner and the radio officer, and try to put the rudder out of action. It probably would not come off, but at least we should have made a fight for it.

For over an hour, we crouched in our uncomfortable positions. It seemed an eternity. Every moment we expected to be hailed and told to heave-to. But our guardian angel was watching over us. The patrol boat appeared to conclude that we were just another fishing vessel returning from a trip, and it passed harmlessly by. I think we all silently offered up a prayer of thanks. I know that I did.

It was now dusk. We had crossed the straits, but we were not yet out of danger. There was a strict rule that all fishing boats and other small craft had to be off the waterways from dusk till dawn. But we could not possibly land anywhere here, and we had still many miles to go before we should reach our first port of call. We would have to sail on during the night and take our chance of being discovered by patrol boats on the prowl. We got another severe fright at seven o'clock when another one loomed up. Down we went on the floor again, and this time our hearts were really thudding, for we felt sure that we should be investigated. But for some reason that I shall never know, we were not. The patrol went by without stopping, and we were able to relax again. It was certainly our lucky day!

Now that we were through the straits, we Australians began to feel safer. Then we noticed that our crew were becoming fidgety and uneasy and we wondered why. After some questioning we discovered the reason for their nervousness. It was not Japs that they were worrying about—it was pirates! They were afraid of a pirate attack. We couldn't help laughing a bit at this. To us, pirates didn't seem much of a danger. When, a little later that night, a cruiser suddenly loomed up ahead of us, a Japanese cruiser, peril from pirates seemed simply nothing at all.

But once more luck was with us. The cruiser was escorting five ships, and evidently thought the danger from submarines was too great for it to be worth her while to stop to investigate the activities of one small fishing boat, even though it was out after prohibited hours. She went by with her convoy, and we breathed again. The rest of the night went by calmly and peacefully and we were able to get some of the sleep we so badly needed after the frightful storm we had endured.

By midday next day we arrived at our first stopping-place, Bargoonan, and, for the time being, were safe. The skipper of our kompit crew lived here, and he entertained us for a couple of days. The people were very kind to us, and gave us fresh fruit and hot coffee and other kinds of food. It made a most acceptable change from our usual diet of rice, bananas, and coconuts. It was good, too, to be able to walk about and stretch our legs. We were entertained at several villages while we were on this island. At one of them, Siokan, we had quite a reception. There was a complete unit of the U.S.F.I.P. here, and its commander, Lieutenant Albert Johnson, came to meet us, invited us to stop at his house for a few days, took us to the officers' mess for meals, and arranged a dance and supper for us, at which we were introduced to some of the prettiest girls I have ever seen. There was a partner for each of us, and though they were rather on the small side and made us feel big and clumsy when we danced with them—I felt like a baby elephant waltzing round with a canary myself—they were all perfectly sweet and charming.

We slept in beds, too, while we were here, and had the comfort of hot baths, and shaving soap, and other luxuries such as we had almost forgotten existed. It seemed as if the people couldn't do too much for us. They seemed to regard us with something more than respect and friendliness—it was

H

almost akin to worship. If any of us expressed the slightest wish for anything, they would move heaven and earth to get it for us if it was in any way obtainable.

The Japanese had not, so far, visited this particular island, and Lieutenant Johnson was making sure that they would not escape quite unharmed if they came. Barriers and obstacles of all types had been erected, and sentries were always posted, in sensible places, too, where they would have a wide vision. A newly-constructed rice mill was surrounded by ground traps, and alarms were fixed so that no enemy could approach without setting one off. We were able to give him a useful tip or two, and in return he gave me a road map of the whole of the southern states. This was, indeed, a treasure, and we both sat down and marked out, between us, every Japanese position of which we knew. This map proved a most valuable asset to me at a later date.

We were very sorry to say goodbye to the people of this hospitable island, when the time came for us to embark once more in our kompit. We left very early in the morning, just as day was dawning, but, early though it was, hundreds of people came down to see us off. The wind was favourable, and under sail we headed out once more to sea.

It was the eleventh of November, Armistice Day. The wind which had brought us out to sea dropped before eleven o'clock, and we kept the Two Minutes' Silence lying becalmed. When it was over, out came the oars, and we started again, in a tropical heat that brought the perspiration pouring out of the rowers. It was pouring out of Jim and me, too, though not from rowing. We had both gone down with malaria again, and were obliged to lie out on the bottom of the boat, shivering and sweating, and sweating and shivering, while the sun scorched down upon us. Our mates did all they could to make us comfortable, but we spent a wretched day. It was a relief to all of us when night came, bringing with it a cooler air. The others did not stop rowing when dark came, but pulled on through the night, taking it in turns to relieve one another at the oars.

During the next few days we continued to move northward, putting in occasionally at an island when our skipper was sure that it was safe to do so. Our next scheduled stopping-place was a village called Sindangan, but a little before we reached it, we stopped at the mouth of a river where there was a small jetty and a cluster of houses, to make inquiries. We had heard a rumour that the Japanese had landed at Sindangan, and thought it wise to find out whether or not it was true before going farther. The skipper, who said that he knew some of the people at this place, went ashore to do the talking. Before leaving us, he warned us not to go into the water while we were waiting, as this particular river was infested with crocodiles. This was enough to put Charlie and Rex who were both dare-devils, on their mettle, and no sooner had he gone than they both jumped in for a quick splash.

The rest of us were on tenterhooks for the next few minutes, going nearly cross-eyed in our efforts to look both ways at once watching for anything that might faintly resemble a floating log. It was a great relief when they came out of the water and we could relax again. The skipper's warning had not been without reason, as we were soon to discover. On the opposite bank of the river from where we were waiting, two natives were trying to persuade two horses to swim across to our side. The horses absolutely refused to do so. They bucked and reared and whinnied, and at last they broke away from their keepers and charged into the jungle. At the same moment, I caught sight of a long ugly snout drifting down the river. The horses had sensed the danger before the humans did. Charlie grabbed a rifle, aimed, and fired. The crocodile, a brute about twenty feet long, leapt up out of the water, turned a complete somersault, and sank.

We were glad, after this, when the skipper returned and we were able to leave. It was true, he told us, that the Japanese had been at Sindangan. They had raided and looted it, but they were not there now and it was safe for us to go on. We experienced another storm while we were making for it, and once more we were tossed about from side to side as our craft battled her way through the raging waters. When we reached our goal we found it impossible to bring the kompit into land, and we were obliged to lower the sail and drop anchor off shore. However, no sooner had we anchored, than several vintas braved the turmoil of the waves and came alongside to bring us to safety. The change over from the kompit to the smaller boats was quite a thrilling experience. No sooner was one of us about the jump when the kompit and the vinta into which he was jumping would be swung apart by the force of the waves and he would be left balanced precariously on the gunwale. However, luck was with us. Not one of us fell into the water, and at length we were all brought safely to shore.

It was dusk when we landed, and in the dim light the village looked a scene of desolation. The Japanese had bombed and raided it heavily. Many houses had been burnt to the ground, others were half-wrecked and their contents looted. Articles too heavy to be moved had been deliberately smashed. A curious instance showing how the Japanese mind worked was that all American pianos were damaged beyond repair, whereas German ones were left untouched. The civilians had all been evacuated into the jungle, and we and the local soldiers were the only persons left in the area. In one spot was a great heap of stolen loot, piled up ready to be taken away. The Japs, we were told, had left it behind because a report had been received that six thousand Australian soldiers had been successfully landed a little farther down the coast and were closing in on Sindangan. This news had caused the enemy to push off in a hurry. Further investigation revealed that those six thousand Australian troops were none other than us seven worn-out, hungry travellers.

It seemed that our timely arrival had done some good after all.

I had my early bath next morning in a newly-formed bomb crater filled with rain water. There were many such pools all over the village, showing how heavy the bombing had been. After breakfast, we wandered round, exploring. Before the Japs came, the village had been well-kept and beautiful. There was a long white beach, bordered on the landward side with rows of waving coconut and paw paw trees. The cottages were well-built, the roads were tarred and well-planned, and in the background were green hills and dense jungle.

The barracks, once a school-house, was a large, two-storied building standing alone in a wide, cleared space. The whole area around this barracks was pitted with bomb holes, but not one had hit the actual building. As at Batu Batu, all had fallen wide of the mark, and it occurred to me that the safest spot during a Japanese raid would be the target itself! But though it had escaped the bombs, the place had not escaped the raiders. Linen and blankets had been burnt, and much valuable equipment destroyed. Much more damage would undoubtedly have been done had it not been for the timely landing of those six thousand members of the Australian contingent!

After we had explored the village, we climbed up to visit an observation post on a high hill. The view from this place was magnificent. To the west were the headlands of a wide, sweeping bay, to the east, green, sloping hills, with rice fields in the valleys and cornfields and well-kept gardens. On the north and south there was jungle, miles and miles of it, housing not only the usual wild jungle animals and reptiles but also many thousands of the civilian population who had taken refuge in it from the invaders. The hill made a splendid site for an observation post, for from it a look-out could be kept over a vast expanse of Japanese-held waters, and timely warning sent to headquarters below. Close by, too, there was a well-camouflaged machine-gun nest, also connected by telephone to H.Q.

While the rest of us were exploring, Charlie and Ray had gone to a village called Siari, to meet two of the senior American-Philippino officers. These men, Lieut.-Col. Tinao and Major Aqunio, had been awaiting our arrival. The next day they both rode back to Sindagan and gave us all a very warm welcome. They told us of the many raids the island had experienced, and of the great damage inflicted, and discussed with us some of the possible plans for our future. For the moment, we were told to follow Charlie and Ray to Siari where hospitality had been arranged for us in the home of Mr. John Roemer, a well-to-do American. We were taken up the coast in a vinta to the village.

Mr. Roemer's home was the most glamorous affair I've ever seen. It was built high up on rising ground and surrounded by beautiful grounds, wide pastures and gardens filled with beautiful flowers and ornamental shrubs. It had been most luxuriously furnished, but it had been visited by the Japs who, as usual, had vented their wrath by smashing up everything they could lay their hands on. Valuable furniture and vases had been broken, and pictures mutilated and slashed. They had tried to fire the house, but fortunately without success, and some sort of order had already been restored to the place. John, as he asked us to call him, treated us like honoured guests. We were given rooms to ourselves, with proper beds, sheets, and pillow-slips, and served with the most wonderful meals. After all we had been through, it felt rather as if we had got to paradise.

Our host was a friendly, genial person, and he regaled us with many good stories, as well as with wonderful food and drink. One tale that I particularly remember concerned a native lad who worked for him. This boy had had a high school education and was considered to be intelligent. John told him to go into the jungle and build a little jungle-house, so that his wife and children—John had a wife and two little girls who had now been evacuated to America—could get to it with ease in case of necessity.

" I told him," said John, " to get some attap out of the store to roof it, and to hurry, and I added : ' And when you have finished it, put a fire stick in it,' meaning of course, that he should lay a fire ready for cooking. And what do you think the brainless idiot did? He put a fire in, right enough—and burned the whole thing down."

" What did you do?" I asked. " Sack him?"

" Sack him? No! I made him go off and build me another one," said John, with a grin.

We spent three nights at John's house, and were taken on our second evening with him to visit a neighbour of his, a Chinese, where we were given " Benty " to drink. It was the first time I had tasted this strange brew. It consisted of beaten up eggs, chocolate, and a drop or two of that high octane stuff—tuba. I thought it quite nice, and there were no ill effects.

The next day, the Colonel, the Major, Ray, Charlie, and Jock, left on horseback for an inland place called Polonko.

The rest of us were to move off the following morning by vinta to another coastal town farther north, from which we could travel to Polonko overland. We left our going as late as we possibly could, for we were very reluctant to say goodbye to this new friend—as I think he was to say goodbye to us, for he begged Jim and me to come back to see him after the war was over. But we had to leave at last, and off we went, moving down by river to the sea in the vinta. We all felt much better for our three days of luxurious living, and we lay back in the boat, smoking, feeling contented and at ease.

Once we were out in the open sea we began to move quickly, for there was a strong wind blowing. Throughout the night we were borne northwards, for the vinta was rather larger than most of these boats and carried a small sail. The waves splashed over us from time to time, and we were soon soaked. My face smarted and my eyes burned from the salt water. Miles and Rex sat with their backs to the bow to avoid having their faces washed so frequently. We made good progress during the hours of darkness, and in the morning we pulled into a little place called Ponot to have our breakfast in calm water.

It was extraordinary how news of our coming went before us in our travels through these islands. The people of Ponot had heard about us, and the moment we touched in they came flocking down to the water's edge to see us, bringing with them gifts of chicken, rice, fruit and carabo's milk. It was the first time I had tasted this milk. It was rather like cow's milk, only richer.

When we pushed off again we found that the wind, strong enough before, had risen to gale force. Our vinta was nearly swamped in the heavy seas, and we had to bail out at top speed all the rest of our voyage. However, in spite of much battering and bailing-out, we arrived safely about six o'clock in the evening at the small coastal town of Dipolog where we were to spend the night before continuing our journey inland to Polonko. The beach looked barren and windswept when we landed, but in a very short time it was crowded with people coming to greet us. The Colonel had told them that we were coming and had asked them to give us a good welcome. They did! Their welcome was simply terrific. The crowds that assembled were staggering, and they cheered and shouted and made us feel as though we were conquering heroes returning from a highly successful war, instead of a party of crocked escaped prisoners. The fact that we were the first Australian soldiers to come to the Philippines may have had something to do with the wonderful receptions we were constantly receiving. But whatever it was, their eager delight at seeing us and the generous hospitality they poured out upon us was heartwarming and moving.

Following that amazing welcome, we were led away from the beach with its rather shabby weather-boarded buildings and conducted over a slight rise to the village itself. This proved to be a most delightful little place. There was a wide, tarred road, a mile long, at the end of which was a cathedral. The houses were large and built according to the best modern tropical standards. Most of them had pretty gardens, attractively laid out, and the whole place was clean and tidy and wore an air of prosperity and contentment. We were taken to the officers' mess—a big room over a large corner shop—where we were given a first-rate dinner. After dinner, the company commander addressed us, telling us that the colonel was giving a welcoming party next day at Polonko, to celebrate our arrival from Tawi Tawi, and that we had better go to bed early, since it would be necessary for us to rise early, in order to get there in time, for we had several miles to travel.

Accordingly we were up to an early breakfast the next morning, and were soon on our way. It was raining slightly, but we did not mind that, it felt so good to stretch our legs again and to have a tarred road to walk upon after the jungle trails to which we were used. After a bit, though, the tarred road came to an end, and once more the going was hard and strenuous, made more so when the rainy drizzle stopped and the sun shone out again in all its tropical heat. Tree trunks had been placed across the road at regular intervals, to form obstacles in case of Japanese invasion, and what with the hot sun and the energy expended in climbing over the trees, we found ourselves obliged to stop for rests more often than we wanted. But at last we reached Polonko, and found it quite a good-sized place with many big buildings. To our surprise, though, it was strangely quiet. There wasn't, at first, a soul to be seen and we wondered what on earth the trouble could be. Then one solitary person appeared in sight and beckoned to us to follow him. We were taken to a room where we found facilities for refreshment and a good wash, and when we had cleaned up and tidied ourselves we were taken to a large hall where we quicky found the reason for the empty streets. Everybody in the place was assembled in that hall! Tables were arranged all round the room, loaded with food and beautifully decorated, and clapping and cheering rose from all sides as we came in. We all felt very bashful. These receptions were something we couldn't get used to. Somehow it seemed all wrong that we should be treated in this wonderful way. It made us feel like impostors, for, after all, all we had done was to escape from hell.

We were put to sit all together, where everybody could see us, and the Colonel made us a speech of welcome. He spoke in glowing terms of our work in Tawi Tawi with the signals which had resulted in the sinking of enemy ships, and he told of our hazardous journey among the islands in enemy-held seas. He concluded by saying that as long as we were in the Philippines he knew that we would do all that we could to help his people in their fight against the murderous Japanese.

The cheers that followed, the clapping and the stamping, were simply deafening. We were all overcome with emotion. Ray, as our senior officer, replied on our behalf. He thanked the Colonel sincerely for the wonderful welcome that we had received, and said that we had only done what, as soldiers, it was our duty to do, and we would continue to do all that we were able in the cause of peace.

It was a marvellous party. A first-class native orchestra played inside the building, and outside a brass band played martial music. The chief tune played by the band was the Regimental March of the 105th Division. This was such a bright, catchy tune that I wrote down the melody, and later recorded it as a piano solo. There was dancing after dinner was done, and in between the dances various artistes sang to us. After a while we Aussies rose as a team and sang as we had never sung before. Some of us were in tune, some of us were out of tune, but nobody cared. Everybody was laughing and happy, and looking round at the faces of my comrades I noted how all the worry and strain of the past months had temporarily disappeared. It was good to see them all enjoying the party so much, laughing and talking almost as though they were back among their loved ones at home. Yet, mingled with my own gladness was a deep sense of sorrow, too, for three faces were missing. Three men that I knew, one that the others knew, Howard Harvey, Daniel MacKenzie, Rex Butler were not there.

We did not stay long in Polonko. The next day Ray went into conference with the Colonel and the Major to plan our future moves, and as a result of their conferring, Jim, Bruce, Sid, and myself were ordered to proceed immediately to hospital in a place called Sibutad. We would have to walk, but we were told that the place was " not far off," and we were allotted a couple of carriers to take our gear, and guides to help us along.

It was ten o'clock in the morning on November the twenty-fifth when our sick party started out. Almost the first thing we had to do was to cross a river by means of a bridge which was primitive in the extreme. It consisted of bamboo poles, floating on the water, tied together with jungle vine. As the water rippled past, so those poles rocked up and down, and I gazed at this ingenious structure with very mixed feelings. It was all right for those light-weight, barefoot natives. They just ran across as though it was the easiest thing in the world. But it was a different matter for us with our bigger build and heavier weight. I sat down and took off my boots, and the other three followed my example. Then Jim set out to negotiate the bridge, while we stood and watched his progress. He moved slowly towards the centre while the bridge swayed and bobbed and sagged beneath him. First his ankles, then his knees were under water, but hiding his fear he went bravely on and reached the other side in safety.

It was my turn next. I had a foreboding as I stepped out that I was going to look ridiculous. The bridge rocked and swung and soon I, too, was up to my knees in water. Then my forboding was realised. A canoe paddled near which set the bridge rocking still more violently and to keep my balance I was forced to bend down and grab the edges with my hands, and the rest of the journey was completed in this ignominious position, creeping along practically on all fours.

Jim was grinning broadly when I finally made the grade and crawled up the bank on the farther side, and the native boys were rocking with merriment. Ignoring what they said, I put on my boots and lit a cigarette while we waited for Bruce and Sid. When they, too, were safely over, we set off on our long trek to that " not far off " hospital. Why they had to put it so far from the town I never could make out, and I wondered how a really sick person, a person too ill to walk, would ever get to it.

We walked along a dirt track, in silence for the most part, for it was too hot to talk much. Banana trees and coconut trees grew beside the trail, and here and there was a farm, or a house with a woman pounding rice in front of it. We stopped for lunch at a small place where there was a market, watched a couple of cock-fights, lost two dollars, and then pushed on again. After what seemed an eternity, we reached the home of Mr. Saguin, now Judge Saguin, Director of Civil Affairs, whose name appears on all the Philippine treasury notes, where we were to spend the night. He and his family did everything possible to make us comfortable. He had a wife and three daughters, who, between them, did all the cooking and housework, as well as a great deal of the gardening.

While we were there Mr. Saguin received some fresh mail, and to my surprise I learnt that in spite of the Japanese occupation of the islands the inhabitants still managed to carry on a secret postal service. The people wrote letters in the usual way, stamped them—I was shown an envelope with a stamp on it marked " Free Philippines Guerilla Postal Service 2 Centavos "—then slipped them into some hollow log to await collection. From these secret post offices they would be picked up, sorted, and sent on their way, by runner, vinta, and kompit, and in this way the islands were kept in touch still with the free world.

Mr. Saguin gave me a signed certificate, to serve as a pass during our travels through the Philippines. It stated that we were Australian and American service men, travelling on official duty in Zamboango Misamis Occidental, and that all Home Guards and loyal civilians were to show us courtesy and give us any assistance that we might need.

In the morning we continued our journey. We had only gone a little way when malaria sruck me again. We found a small cottage where I could rest for the acute stage, and Bruce and one of the guides stayed with me, while Jim and Sid went ahead. As soon as the sweating period was over we went on again. We had been calling our guide "Darling" because that was the name his wife had called him, but during that day's march we felt that it was not a very appropriate name for him. He was exasperating in the way he kept telling us that we had not much farther to go, that the hospital was "Near, very near," when all the time it was still miles distant. "About two cigarillos," he would tell us, meaning the time it would take to smoke two cigarettes. We reckoned that those cigarettes must have been mighty big ones, unless he allowed about seven miles between the two smokes. Mile after mile we struggled on in the heat. Sometimes we were clambering up a mountain side, the next minute we were dropping down into a gloomy valley, with another uphill climb directly ahead. It seemed an endless walk, and we were in no mood to appreciate the lovely flowers and beautiful sights around us.

However, all things come to an end at last, and even that walk ended. We came to a small river, across which we waded, and there, in a clearing, was the hospital. Bruce and I heaved sighs of relief as we scrambled up to it, and in a very short while we both found ourselves in bed.

Dr. Caesar Ingles was in charge of the hospital. He came to examine us at once, and then detailed orderlies to care for us. Beyond being put to bed and fed, given a little massage and doped with various medicines, not much was done to us that night. But the next day treatment began in earnest. We were all fumigated, and blood tests were taken to decide exactly what types of malaria we each had. Hidden in the bush nearby was a laboratory, to which the slides were taken. Even here there was need for concealment, for the Japanese came from time to time, raiding and looting, and trying to kill or capture members of the Resistance Movement. I was told that they had paid a visit to the hospital only a short time before, but one of the male nurses had succeeded in saving a large quantity of medicines and other supplies, and they had not found much to carry off.

The rest and relaxation soon made me feel better, and in a day or two both Jim and I were walking about. Dr. Ingles asked me if I would instruct some of the students he was training in map-reading while I was staying in hospital, which I at once agreed to do. Jim was roped in to help in repairing the damage the Japs had done to the distillery. We were both pleased to have jobs to occupy our time now that we were no longer bed patients, for we would have to remain where we were for some little time yet. Jim's blood tests showed him to be, temporarily, all clear, though he would still need treatment. Mine were rather worse than his—" Malignant Malaria, Type ' Tertian,' " my card read.

We received a message from some of our friends while we were in hospital. It was brought in by a native runner, and it warned us to be very careful where we went and to whom we spoke. The Japs knew about our small party and a substantial reward had been offered for our capture. Especially for us Australians!

" Australians are to be skinned alive," the runner told us cheerfully.

Extra guards were placed all round the area after the receipt of this warning. I can't say that this made us feel much safer. We remembered some of the guards at Tawi Tawi and the way they had behaved when the enemy came, and we prayed fervently that these might be made of sterner stuff.

Meanwhile our medical treatment went on, and we began to feel better. We had a few setbacks, of course. One morning, we were given squid for breakfast, a delicacy which the natives love, but which thoroughly upset Bruce and me. Another time Dr. Ingles told us that the people of a neighbouring village wanted to give a party in our honour. It was only about twenty minutes' walk away, he said, and there was only one stream to cross. He thought we were fit enough to accept the invitation. So, trusting to his judgment, we set off. After crossing three streams and walking for an hour and a half, we arrived at our destination, almost too tired to talk. The party was really wonderful, but it came on to rain so hard that we had to stay the night. When we got back to hospital the next morning, Jim and I had both of us to be put to bed on a light diet with another dose of malaria.

Bruce and Sid were discharged from hospital on December the fifth, and returned to Polonko. Jim and I had to stay for another few days before we were judged fit to go out. We did not mind, as we were both busy and occupied doing our respective jobs for the doctor. My map-reading class was making real progress by this time. The students were doing a road traverse, learning to scale distances, and graphing their attempts on paper. I felt very pleased with them.

On December the tenth, we were told that we were well enough to leave, and we packed up our traps, ready to make an early start the next morning. In the evening Dr. Ingles invited us to go for a stroll with him. We both went with him unsuspectingly, and he took us to the clearing station, were, to our surprise, we found that the whole of the hospital staff was gathered to wish us goodbye. It was quite a party. There were refreshments, and singing and dancing, and at the end, when Jim and I had to go, one of the students gave a signal and the whole company, nurses, orderlies, cooks, and medicos, lined up to form a guard of honour, and as we moved off broke into one of the songs they had learnt from us, *Leave Us With A Smile*.

It was all most moving. I almost wondered if I was going to faint, I felt so overcome. I was glad it was the end of the party, for I had such a lump in my throat that, if I had tried to speak, I should have burst into tears. As we made our way back to our beds, I thought that it was no wonder that we loved these people. With their gaiety, and hospitality, and true generosity, they must surely be the most lovable race in the world.

CHAPTER IX

ON THE MOVE AGAIN

O n t h e eleventh of December, 1943, we left the hospital, and with our carriers and a guide we headed back over the streams and the mountain ranges to Polonko. The trip back did not seem to be nearly so long as the journey coming out, I suppose because we were both so much better in health. When we reached Polonko, we found that Colonel Tanio had taken Ray, Charlie, Rex, Miles, and Jock, to the divisional headquarters. Major Aqunio had been left in charge at Polonko, so we reported to him, and he told us that we were to rest for a day or two, and then we were to go to join the others.

Bruce and Sid were very glad to see us arrive. They had been waiting impatiently for us to come, for they wanted to get going, and the powers that be had decided that they must wait for us, so that the one set of guides could do for the four of us. They were not kept waiting much longer. On the morning of December the sixteenth, the party was ready to start. It consisted of us four, together with the Major, his wife and seven children, and nineteen guides and carriers. It was not going to be a luxury trip. There were no horses, there was hardly even a trail. We would have to make our way on our own feet through wild country, over rivers and mountain ranges, and through bogs and jungle to our destination, an unknown number of miles away. We all knew that it was going to be something of a hair-raising adventure, though just how difficult the going was to prove, none of us four guessed.

127

We started off, the Major leading. He was a very fine man, a thorough gentleman, tall and fit, and good-looking, intelligent, and efficient in addition to possessing a great sense of humour. As we were to discover, his energy and resource were endless. To begin with, we were all in a very good temper. We were walking along a level road, bordered by trees and flowering shrubs, and we laughed and talked as though we hadn't a care in the world. Then, rounding a bend, we found before us a wide river which had to be crossed. There was no bridge, there were not boats, so taking off our boots we started to wade across, the water almost waist-deep at times. The Major's smaller children had to be carried across.

That river was only the beginning. By the time we stopped at midday for lunch, we had taken off our boots and put them on again four times. The sun was scorching, there wasn't a cloud in the sky, and we were out in open country for the most part, with paddy fields all around us, and practically no shade. By the end of the first day, we had crossed ten rivers and covered about fourteen miles.

We stayed that first night in a house in a small place called Milad. There was no singing or talking that evening. As soon as we had eaten, we just lay down and went to sleep, we were all so tired. When we woke in the morning we had breakfast, and watched the lady of the house at work at her weaving machine. She was a little wrinkled old lady, sucking a pipe which must have been nearly as old as herself, and she took no notice of anybody as she sat plodding away, turning abaca threads, from abaca skins, into a kind of cloth. Outside the house, men were making rope, using a simple device consisting of three capstans, to which long fibres were attached, with wheels that spun round twisting the rope into shape.

Our route on this second day was along a mountain trail. It was treacherous and slippery, with potholes here and there, three or four feet deep, and filled with black mud. There was great amusement whenever one of the company slipped into one of these holes and came out covered with mud. There was a great deal of climbing to be done. Often we had to creep on hands and knees to reach the summit of some particularly steep peak. And when we got to the top we would have to descend into a ravine, only to start climbing up again directly we got to the bottom. The peaks were often only a stone's throw apart, yet to get from one to the other meant hours of climbing.

By lunch-time that second day we had " had it." We had reached a little " All-Weather House," and we were all so tired that we decided to stay there until the next morning. The house was raised from the ground on piers, and reached by a jungle-made ladder. It had no walls and very little roof, but it was a place where we could rest our tired bodies and we were thankful to reach it. It stood on the bank of a shallow river, which we found a great blessing. We all found relief in bathing, and those who had fallen into potholes were able to wash the mud away.

The next morning it was raining, but there was no sense in staying where we were since there was not enough roof to afford us any shelter, so we decided to get going. But it was a nightmare of a journey that day. The rain pelted down, visibility was almost nil, and the trail wandered about over mountains and through jungles in the craziest fashion. I thought that a good name for it would be Maniac trail, since only maniacs would dare to use it. We crossed rivers too numerous to count, there were fallen trees and slippery rocks to be surmounted, and all the while we had to be on the look-out for scorpions and snakes and other deadly creatures, and endure the torments of attacks from leeches and mosquitoes.

Our guide cheered us on with the usual remarks; " Not far, sir," " Quite near," and other reassuring statements. I made a rough calculation and said to Bruce:

" I suppose that means about another four miles." Bruce was too tired to answer. He just plodded on, lifting one leaden foot after the other. I had lost the sole of one of my boots, and my feet and legs were aching terribly. Even the Major's tireless children showed signs of fatigue, and when we arrived at a place called Sibulan, we decided to stay and turn in early and get a good long sleep. We didn't get it, though, partly because we were all over-tired, and partly because the building allotted to us was full of cockroaches, who did a war-dance up and down the floor all night. The tapping noise

I

they made was like an army tattoo played on kettledrums, and it never ceased for a moment, with the result that when it was time to get up, we were more tired than when we lay down.

We were all so exhausted that the Major decreed we should spend the day where we were and try to get some rest, for the guide had informed us that the next stage of the journey would be " long and tedious." What exactly this meant we didn't know, but it caused us a good deal of foreboding in view of the distance " Near " and " Very near " meant to the native. When we set off at about five o'clock the next morning, the guide told us encouragingly: " Not too far there-o " which so exasperated me that I could have shot him then and there if he hadn't been the only guide we had and without him we would have been lost.

The trails on this day were terrific. It was the only word for them. They were wet and slippery and very dangerous. They wound up hill through dense jungle to the top of steep mountains, only to drop several thousand feet on the other side. Often the slopes were so steep that we had to dig holes with knives so that we could get some sort of foothold. This, of course slowed down our progress considerably, and in order to avoid having to spend the night in the jungle we had to cut out meals and push on without stopping.

Nightmare isn't the word to describe that day's journey! Some of the obstacles we had to negotiate were enough to turn anybody's hair grey. At one place we had to cross a deep gorge bridged by a huge tree which had fallen across it many years before. We crossed one by one, most of us down on hands and knees. As I crawled over I looked down and saw below a river, racing over rocks and foaming against great boulders, and I became suddenly scared and began to feel giddy. I had hastily to lift my eyes and fix them on the other side, not daring to look down again. The whole procedure was nerve-racking, and we were all thankful when we reached the other side in safety. As we sat, trying to recover from our ordeal, the guide told us that many lives had been lost in this crossing. I think we were all a little white as we listened to his stories, and we grew whiter still as we watched the Major's children run across the tree trunk as fearlessly as if they were on a level road.

After we had rested and our blood pressure had returned to normal, we prepared to tackle the next problem. This was to scale a peak which was almost as steep as the side of a house. Climbing it was rather like swarming up a flagpole. When at last we got to the top I did not so much as sit down, I fell down, completely done in. Seeing how exhausted we were, the Major did allow us a brief rest period here. During the rest, one of the carriers shot a monkey, so for our next meal we had some fresh meat as a change from the perpetual rice. It tasted a little like rabbit, only it was much tougher. Still, we enjoyed it all the same.

We stopped that night in a little school house at Simita. It was terribly dirty, but it was so lovely to be able to lie down and sleep, that none of us minded the dirt. But the night was not nearly long enough for me. Major Aqunio was a regular glutton for punishment. He had us up and off at daybreak. Jim and I plodded along together, too tired even to talk. On and on we went, hour after hour, following a winding trail that turned and twisted in every direction. We reached Pana-gan by lunch time and were given our meal in the gaol, a large stockade erection, made from bamboo. I wished that they would keep me there for a few days—even gaol would seem like paradise in my exhausted condition. But no such luck! Without allowing us time for even an' after-dinner smoke, the Major had us on our aching feet again and off once more we set.

After leaving the gaol house, the trail took us through long grass which concealed innumerable mud holes made by carabo, the big animals that look like buffalo. It was often impossible to avoid these holes, one stepped into them before one realised that they were there. Often the mud came up to our knees, sticky, black mud that dropped down from our legs and squelched out of our boots with ever step we took. Our progress, owing to these mud holes, was very slow, and we all looked like a party of nigger minstrels before the day was done. Fortunately there were no more mountains to climb, though when it came to choosing between them and the

Carabo Trail, as the mud-hole track was called by the natives, there really wasn't much to choose.

About 5 p.m. we reached a place named Paraisan where we were met by the Divisional Quartermaster. I don't know what he thought of us all. We were certainly a sight to see—and smell! We longed for baths to wash off the horrible mud, but we were not to have the pleasure of them yet. We still hadn't arrived at our destination, and were to spend the night here, but it was hopeful to see the Quartermaster.

" After all," I pointed out to the others. " A quartermaster wouldn't be so very far away from his headquarters. We must really now be getting ' Very Near '."

This thought cheered us all up no end.

Again there was no talking after our evening meal. As soon as it was over we all settled down to sleep. We did not get nearly as much as we wanted, though. Early in the morning some fowls started their early-rising songs, and thereafter the clucking of the hens and the crowing of the rooster made sleeping impossible. We staggered out to breakfast, half-awake, and were told by our guide that we really were " Very near " now. One more hour, he said, and we should be at H.Q.

" One hour!" I said to Jim. " If we multiply it by five, divide the sum by the number in our party, then multiply the result by the fowls in the yard, maybe we should get an idea of the time we'll arrive at our destination."

We left at 7 a.m. Only one hour to go! Bruce, who was now full of spirit, led the way. We hardly needed the guide now, for the way was clear enough, trampled and wide. But there were still those deep, muddy holes in which the carabo were in the habit of lying down and wallowing. They did it to protect themselves from the vicious carabo fly, for when they were covered with a thick coat of mud, they were safe from the pest. Bruce began to sing *I'm Happy When I'm Hiking*, but he had only got as far as " I'm happy " when he suddenly disappeared out of our sight. He had stepped into one of the carabo holes, an extra deep one. He couldn't get out by himself and we had to fish him out with the help of long poles. He was a sight to see when we at last extracted him, covered with black mud from head to foot, and smelling to high heaven.

After that episode, apart from a few sniggers when we looked at Bruce, we progressed in silence. We were glad to arrive at the next river, for we were all pretty muddy by that time. We sat down in the water, clothes and all, and lay there hoping that the swift running current would wash away some of the mud and smell. By the time we had finished bathing it was eleven o'clock. That hour was passing.

On we went again, tired and wet and thoroughly disheartened. Still, it couldn't be long now, I thought, and fixed my eyes on a small rise ahead of us. When we had surmounted that, perhaps we should be in sight of the end of our journey. On and on we went, across two creeks, over fallen trees, through a maze of scrub and undergrowth, and then we began to climb the slope. It was steeper than it had looked from the distance, and the trail was very slippery. For every foot we climbed, we would slip back two, as often as not. We had to make use of trees and bushes and vines, pulling ourselves up by means of our hands before at last we reached the summit.

There a welcome sight awaited us. Ahead of us there was a wide clearing with buildings. Really only a " little way " to go now! And at 5 p.m., after ten hours on the road, we reached the end of that " One Hour's " journey.

We four, Bruce, Jim, Sid, and myself, reported to Colonel Tanio soon after we reached 105 Divisional Headquarters. We looked a comical picture of misery, and the Colonel doubled up with laughter at the sight of us. Dirty, wet, unshaven, our clothing tattered and torn and caked with mud, we certainly did not look much like Australian and American servicemen reporting to Divisional H.Q. The soldiers who were all about stared at us wide-eyed as we passed them, as though we were wild animals escaped from the jungle. Well, we had certainly come through it—and we were all too thankful to have reached our destination to worry about what anybody thought.

We learned that a large party of soldiers were leaving this place very shortly to go across the bay, Panigurin Bay, to join another section of the unit which was stationed there. Charlie, Ray, Miles, Rex, and Jock, were over the bay with that section, and after a few days' rest, we were to go over to them and join in whatever it was they were doing. We learned, too, that only a few miles away, there was a Japanese garrison, complete with planes and ships, and the usual camp followers. We could catch a glimpse of this Japanese strong-hold from where we now were, and we realised that once again we were vulnerable to the bombing attacks and raids from which we had for some time been protected.

After a good hot bath apiece, and a first-class meal in pleasant surroundings, we sat down with cigarettes to read the latest war news. Things had altered considerably since we last heard any outside news, and it felt good to be in the picture again, especially since the news was so much better. There was no sitting up late for any of us that night. We were aching with tiredness, and we got off to bed as early as we could to get a good long sleep.

I was still terribly tired when I awoke next morning. My body was sore all over, aches and pains everywhere, too numerous to mention. My eyes, too, were very bad. However, I felt better after a good shower. Showers are a wonderful idea for these hot countries. While Bruce was enjoying one, I remarked that it was rather different from the bath he had taken in the carabo hole the previous day. Whereupon he threw the soap at me. We had recovered our spirits, anyway, even if our bodies were still a little the worse for wear.

The barracks were well equipped in every way. In addition to the main buildings there were many smaller ones, for soldiers' quarters, kitchens, toilets, and showers. A little way off, in the jungle, was a hospital and a radio station. As well as picking up ordinary broadcasts, the radio station could send and receive messages. On December the twenty-third, a mes-sage was received saying that the Japanese had made a successful landing across the bay, where our friends were. We were very worried when we heard this news, and wondered if it was just a routine raid, or if, perhaps, the Japs had heard that our pals were there and were after them. We knew, from their having offered a reward for our capture that they were aware we were in the neighbourhood. We wished that we were with our mates, but as it was, all that we could do was to sit about and wait to see what happened.

Time that day went very slowly as we waited for further news. There was a break in the waiting period when a party of boys and girls, dressed up in fancy clothes and accompanied by their parents, arrived to sing Christmas carols to the soldiers. They had a banjo with them and they sang all the familiar tunes, known in Christian countries the whole world over. Suddenly, they started to sing *Holy Night, Silent Night,* and I felt as though somebody had knocked me down. This tune hurts me more than anything else I know. It brings back such memories, bitter, hateful memories of Sandakan and all the horrors that took place there. It hurt me so much that day that I could not stay to listen to it, but slipped off on my own. Nobody else here knew all that I knew about the prison camp. Most of what we had endured was to be kept secret until I was back in Australia and could reveal it to the right people, people who would know how much of the horrors it would be wise to make public. But I could not stay to listen to that tune. As I moved away I thought of Frank. Was he alive? Was he well? And Joo Meng? How was he, and how were all the other men I knew? Visions of last Christmas rose before me,—those visions, I know, will always be with me at Christmas time, because that tune will always be sung at Christmas, and whenever I hear it my thoughts will fly back.

Later that afternoon Jim and I took a stroll to look at the local market. There was nothing to see in it that we had not already seen dozens of times in all the towns and villages we had visited in the Philippines. There were the usual fruit and vegetables, the cakes and scones, and fruit drinks, the usual cock fights. But we were glad to get away from army routine for a while, and I, for my part, was especially glad to get away from carols. Jim and I were usually to be found together, and the next day we set off to visit the village of Boni-Facio, which one of the soldiers told us was " Not too far away." Jim and I grinned at each other as we heard the familiar phrase. But we thought we might as well go there.

It could not, we thought, be more than ten miles, and what were ten miles to us who had just travelled hundreds?

The trails were like most of those we had encountered, the sun was as hot as ever, but we were used to these things by now, and it was pleasant to hear the birds singing and to see the butterflies fluttering from tree to tree. Except for our worry about our friends on the other side of the bay, we felt happy and relaxed. We meant to take two days over our journey, and could stroll along at our ease. We rested whenever we wanted to, and when we came across water, we sat and cooled our feet. I was especially glad of that, for my boots were quite worn out, and I was obliged to go barefooted.

In spite of all our stops, we got to Boni-Facio by one o'clock. We were welcomed to the village by Father Cronin, the parish priest. He asked us if we would like some good cigarettes.

" Sure we would," we told him, adding : " But where can we get such luxuries in these wartime days?"

" You wait," said the Father, and he walked into his house and came out wearing a broad grin on his face and carrying in his hand a brand new full packet of *Lucky Strike* cigarettes. It was a wonderful present for Jim and me for we seldom had a really good cigarette to smoke these days. Father Cronin's generosity was not ended. Noticing my bare feet, he asked me what size boots I took, and when I said eights he went off and returned with a pair of size eight shoes. I was quite speechless for a moment or two, but when I recovered from my surprice I poured out my thanks.

Jim was invited to spend the night with the priest, and I was asked to the house of a Chinese. I was given a great time and made very comfortable. We had singing in the evening, and I sang a solo which received quite an ovation when I had finished—perhaps because it *was* the end.

The next day was Christmas Day. I wondered if the Japanese thought of it as we do, as a day of goodwill towards men. Remembering Sandakan it was difficult to believe that they did. We had to start on our return journey, but we wanted to say goodbye to Father Cronin before we went, so we stood by the church waiting for the service he was taking to finish. While we waited, I was startled to hear the *Blue Danube* being played on the church organ. I asked Father Cronin when he came out if I had heard correctly, and he laughed and told me that I had, adding: " It does not worry me. I never do anything about such things."

He wanted us to spend the day with him, but we had to get off, so we said goodbye and left him with regret. We should have been glad to stay longer with him, but we were both anxious about what was going on across the bay, and felt that we must get back, so as to be on hand if we were wanted. Before leaving the village, I bought two school exercise books and a box of matches, and was startled to find that I had to pay ten shillings in our money for them.

Sad news awaited us on our return. As we reached H.Q. we were met by Ray who had come back from the other side of the bay. We knew from his face that there was something wrong, and as we hurried to meet him he told us that Lieutenant Charles Wagner had been killed. He had been picked off by a Japanese sniper, near the bridge in the Liangan district, directly opposite to the occupied island of Misamis. This was tragic news, and Jim and I were stunned with dismay when we heard it. It was hard to believe that our cheerful, happy-go-lucky pal, Charlie, had gone.

Ray told us that their unit had been attacked in a surprise raid, the guards having failed to give any warning. Practically everything the unit possessed had been lost—books, stores, army gear. The Japs had not stayed for reprisals. As soon as they had struck their blow they had made off again, but the damage had been done and Charlie was dead. I recalled how the guards at Tawi Tawi had rushed off into the jungle without warning us when the Japanese had landed there, and I realised how difficult it was to rely upon these lovable but rather unstable people.

As things had quietened down across the bay, Ray went back, but we were told to wait where we were until we got further orders. This made us all rather on edge, for we wanted to go and see what was happening, to help if we could. However, I went down with another turn of malaria while we waited, so it was just as well I was where I was. I was nursed by a female nurse this time, a girl with a winsome smile and curves all in the right places. She nursed me so well and gave me so much attenion that I soon recovered and was shot out of the hospital in next to no time. When I got back to the others I hoped that we might have been sent for to go to Ray, but I found that there had been a radio message from him, telling us to stay where we were for the time being.

We spent a dismal New Year's Eve. There were no celebrations at all, and we all went early to bed, praying that the New Year would bring peace to the troubled world and take us home.

The next morning, January 1st, 1944, a special parade was held to hear a message from General McArthur, who at that time was in the New Guinea area, gradually working his way back to the Philippines. This man was a great hero to the Philippinos, who loved and trusted him implicitly. In the radio message that New Year's Day, he told them that he would return to them in the very near future and free their country from the Japanese.

Jim and I were offered full-time positions with the Division, with a promise of much senior rank. But we both refused the offer. I was still ill, not only with malaria. I had a double hernia, and knew that I must get somewhere where I could get proper treatment for it as soon as possible. Also I had promised Frank to deliver many messages for him, and I wanted to tell those in authority about the terrible conditions in the Sandakan camp in the hope that it might be possible to do something about them. Jim, too, declined for many good reasons.

As still no orders came from the other side of the bay, I sent two radio messages to Colonel Bowler who was the C.O. there, asking if we could not cross over to them. No reply came to either message, and we grew more and more worried about our mates. At last we decided to take the matter into our own hands and not wait for orders any longer. On January the fifth, I sent a third message, not asking this time, but stating firmly that we were crossing over, and without wasting any more time, Jim, Bruce, Sid, and myself, with a party of signallers set off for the water front to get transport to take us to the other side of the bay.

CHAPTER X

AT GENERAL HEADQUARTERS

Our journey down to the coast was the easiest we had had for many a day, although we did have to cross sixteen small streams and climb a few medium-sized hills. But on the whole the going was good, and we reached Panguit, the waterside village where we hoped to get a boat, about seven o'clock in the evening.

The village lieutenant, or " Barrio " as he was termed, was the owner of the boat which would take us across the bay. He arranged a meal for us, and said that he hoped to leave about ten that night. But when the time came and we went down to have a look at the water we found it far too rough to attempt a crossing, and the trip had to be postponed until the following morning. At 7 a.m. we four, together with the crew and about twenty-two other people who wanted to cross, went on board a large vinta, and as soon as the skipper came we pushed off.

The sea still looked rather rough, but it was not thought to be too bad, and a sail was hoisted. Everything went well as long as we were in the shelter of the little cove from which we had started, but once we were away from its protective cover, things began to grow frightening. The wind was much stronger than had been expected, and the vinta simply bowled along before it. Soon it was blowing a gale. The waves came over the top of the boat again and again, and I began to feel very worried. I confided my fears to Jim, but he remarked that the Admiral, as we called the skipper, seemed to know what he was doing and that everything would probably be all right. Bruce and Sid appeared to be as anxious as I was, but the Admiral told us not to worry. The boat, he said, was unsinkable, which reassured us for the time being.

Faster and faster the boat flew before the wind which now increased to almost hurricane force. The vinta was tossed up and down, often at an angle of sixty degrees. Water came swamping in, and as fast as we baled it out, in it flooded again. We were hanging on now to anything we could catch hold of, and we were all seriously alarmed. I managed to remove my boots and most of my clothes, so as to be ready for an emergency which I felt sure must come.

Sure enough it did. We had travelled about half way across the bay when a huge wave struck us, broadside on. The boat gave a sickening lurch, and then another huge wave came thundering down upon us, completely filling the boat with water. She did not sink, it was true, the skipper was right so far. But she was submerged and remained so, with her structure under water, and the only thing showing above the surface her mast.

We four, I am glad to say, retained our heads, but the crew and the rest of the passengers panicked, and we had our work cut out to control them. We did our best to encourage them, telling them to hold on tight to whatever they could even if it was to something below water. I sent one of the lads up the mast to see if any help was on the way, but the only thing he could see was a Japanese patrol boat, which added to everybody's terror. I tried to console them by pointing out that though we could see the patrol boat, they were very unlikely to see us in these mountainous seas because only our mast was above water.

" Try and forget about the Japs," I said.

The seas continued to rage about us, at the same time the sun blazed down on us, scorching us painfully. We were tossed to and fro, and spun round and round, while we all clung on like grim death to the framework of the vinta. I swallowed several mouthfuls of water, which caused me to vomit violently. The others were mostly in the same condition. As the minutes turned into hours we all became thoroughly exhausted, and I wondered how much longer any of us would be able to hold on.

Then suddenly a new terror was added to our situation. Something brushed past my leg, and sent a thrill of horror through my veins. My God, I thought, are there sharks here? I looked to see if anyone else had had the same experience, and saw from the sickly expression on Bruce's face that he had felt something too. I gave him a quick warning to say nothing, for I knew that if the natives realised that there were sharks about they would lose their heads completely and would probably bring about the end for us all.

I sent another boy up the mast and gave him my shirt, telling him to wave it and try to attract attention from the shore, but warning him not to do so if the patrol was still in sight. He managed to reach the top of the mast, despite the way it swayed from side to side, and looked about him.

" For God's sake don't make any mistake," Jim screamed up to him. " Don't wave to the Japs whatever you do."

The patrol was not in sight, and the lad waved frantically, clinging perilously to the mast with one hand while he gripped the shirt in the other. Then another huge wave made the boat give a violent lurch. His grip relaxed for a moment, and the shirt was torn from his hand and carried away by the wind.

Looking the picture of misery, the boy came down from the mast. He tried to say he was sorry, and I told him that it couldn't be helped and the loss of the shirt didn't matter. But I was rather dumbfounded when he said :

" And please, sir, may I borrow your comb?"

Jim and Bruce went off into fits of laughter, and the little incident did us all good. It struck us as so funny that he could bother about what his hair looked like at a time like this.

Another hour passed slowly away, and all the while our fear grew greater. There was no disguising the fact now that sharks were in the vicinity. We could see them in the distance, small black dots, growing larger as they made their way towards us, sometimes visible, sometimes swallowed up by the waves. Then, suddenly, help came. Our signal had been seen from the shore, and several vintas had been sent to our assistance by the barrio lieutenant, and almost before we could believe our eyes, we were being helped aboard them by our rescuers.

Except that Bruce and I were pitched out of the first vinta we boarded and had to swim to another one, the transfer went off without a hitch, and very soon we were safely on land. Many people were waiting to receive us and they seemed as relieved as we were ourselves when we all stepped ashore. We were on the right side of the bay, but not yet quite where we wanted to be. I got a message off, though, to Colonel Bowler, reporting what had happened and saying that we hoped to get to him in the course of a few days.

The villagers were very good to us. They lit fires and helped us to wash and dry out clothes, and we spent that night with them. The next day, though, we four moved further inland. It would be safer, both for us and for the villagers, if we were not too near the coast should the Japs make another surprise landing. The barrio lieutenant roped two vintas together, and we headed into a small river and moved upstream.

My malaria had started up again, and we had not got far on our way when I was prostrate with it. Jim got off the boat and went prospecting and made friends with a kindly family named Soques who lived near by, and they agreed to take me in. Mr. Soques came back to the boat with Jim, and I was helped to his house and put to bed. A few days of rest and careful nursing put me right and I was soon on my feet again. I could only thank Mr. Soques for his kindness. I had nothing to give him—no money, no possessions except the water-stained clothes I was wearing—nothing but thanks.

As soon as I was fit enough to travel, Jim and I set off to try and make contact with Colonel Bowler's unit. Mr. Soques's house was on the outskirts of the village of Lalla and we had to pass through the village when we left. There were the usual market-place, surrounded by cottages, and the school. I noticed that the school was larger than usual and that the grounds were very wide, wide enough for a plane to land on them and take off again. I thought this might be a useful bit of information to hand on to the right people and made a mental note of it.

It was rather a nightmare of a walk for me, for my legs and back were aching from the fever, my eyes were burning, and my head throbbed. I struggled on for a while, when we were lucky enough to come across a horse-drawn carriage known as a calassie. It was a queer kind of contraption, but I needed a lift too badly to mind about that, so we pulled up the driver and asked him to take us to Baroy where we hoped to get a vinta which would take us along the coast to H.Q. We had no money which made bargaining difficult, but after some argument the driver agreed to take us in exchange for an I.O.U., and after a long and tedious journey we got to Baroy.

Here we hired a vinta, with the help of another I.O.U. and set off again, wondering if our I.O.U's would be honoured by the Army. If they were, all would be well—if not, our names would be mud! However, we felt that it was the only thing to do. Moving along the coast, we were startled to see that only about three miles away from us was the Japanese base on the island of Misamis. We had not known that it was quite so near. However, we passed safely by, and reaching Liangan we reported to Colonel Bowler.

We found Ray, Miles, Rex and Jock, comfortably established at Headquarters. They were very surprised to see us walk in, for my *first* radio message had only reached them that morning. Jim and I were angry and concerned. If it took all that time to receive a radio message, there must be something very wrong with the organisation. It was no wonder that the Japanese raid had taken them by surprise. There was no room for us to stay permanently at headquarters, but we were allowed to spend the night in the office, where we took turns in sleeping, one or the other of us staying awake to keep watch. We neither of us felt much trust in the guards, and we were determined not to fall again into Japanese hands, if we could possibly help it.

In the morning we were given a hundred dollars and told to find ourselves some hiding-place until a sail boat was ready to take us to Butuan which might not be for some days yet. We decided that we would go back to Lalla and see if Mr. Soques would take us in again. He seemed very pleased to see us and gladly agreed to do so. We were able to give him the latest news which was good, and this cheered him up immensely. For the next few days we took life easily, wandering about the village, and exploring the empty houses which had been damaged by bombs or in the hit-and-run raids. We found the people on this side of the bay brighter and healthier than those on the other, probably due to the better food. There was abundance of food in this side, corn and meat, instead of the rice and fish which was the staple diet on the other. Indeed, the whole place seemed so prosperous, with its own rice mill, and its plentiful supplies of pigs, cattle, carabo, horses, corn, and fish, that Jim and I both thought it was extremely likely that the Japanese would raid it again in the near future. When Mr. Soques took us to see a chemical-distillery which was in operation nearby in the jungle, turning high octane tuba into a super-power alcohol for running motor trucks and launches, our forebodings were increased. The dispenser in charge of the distillery, who was a Russian, said that he was producing fifteen gallons a day, and could do a good deal better if the labour position improved.

On the seventeenth of January, Jim and I were sitting on the veranda of Mr. Soques's house, having a quiet smoke, when a runner arrived from Colonel Bowler to tell us to return at once to H.Q. Saying goodbye to our kind host, we set off immediately, following the same trail as before, and duly reported. We were then sent to the officers' mess to spend the night. The next day, we were told, the big sail boat was due and we would start on the first stage of our journey home.

The next morning, after a hurried breakfast, we went down to the river, where there was anchored the biggest sailing-boat I had ever seen. Outside in the bay, there were two Japanese patrol boats, but they dared not come into attack, for the sailing boat was well armed. She had two .5 millimetre and two 30 millimetre cannon, besides numerous anti-aircraft guns, tommy guns, rifles and carbines. In fact, she was practically a floating arsenal.

Stores and equipment were being unloaded from the boat when we arrived, guns and ammunition, boots, radio gear,

and boxes of comforts. Rex Blow was there, so the three of
us sat down to have a talk while we waited. Rex tried to
persuade us to stop with them. Colonel Bowler had asked him
to do so. He said that all the others were going to stay, and
we should both get advancement if we did, too. But we
refused, and explained to him why we felt that we must
get home to Australia if it were possible. We were both in
very bad health and needed proper medical attention, and
promotion would be useless to us if we were going to be
really ill. And, besides, I had my private reasons for wanting
to get back. There were still those prisoners at Sandakan,
suffering such terrible ill-usage, and I felt that I must see
if anything could be done to help them. Even if nothing
could, I must at least let those in authority in Australia
know what was happening.

After a while Colonel Hedges came down to the river,
and told us not to go far away. The orders about sailing had
not yet arrived, but he expected to receive them soon after
lunch, and we must be on hand so as not to miss our chance.
We found that we should have to provide our own food, and,
since we had no money, we were obliged to sell some of our
few possessions in order to buy a meal. A pleasant surprise
came along while we were waiting. Bruce, Sid, and four other
Americans arrived from their hiding-place to go with us when
the boat sailed. It cheered us up a lot to know that we should
have companions.

But we were in for a bad disappointment. During the wait,
a Moro Datu—a head tribesman—beckoned to me to come
to him, and when I went to see what he wanted he took
a ring of beaten silver, with a fossil set in its centre, from
his finger and tried to put it upon one of mine. An interpreter
told me that it was the ring of office, and the Datu wanted
me to keep it as a token of the friendship he and all his tribe
felt for us. While I was talking to him, I suddenly heard
the sail-boat's engines begin to turn over, and before I or any
of the others could do anything it began to move off.

We stood gaping in amazement, hardly able to believe our
eyes. Surely, it was not going off without us? We rushed
down to the water's edge, where we were told that we did not

K

need to worry, as the boat was only going round the headland to Esperanso, where it would re-victual, and would then return for us after dark. Sid, however, was uneasy and raced through the jungle to Esperanso where he got on board. The rest of us, however, stayed where we were, hoping that the boat would return as promised. Hour after hour we waited, then a message came from Colonel Bowler telling me that the boat would be late, and that, when it did come, I was to hold it until Father King and a Mr. Redding, who were going to join us, had arrived. This made us feel a little better, and we sat up all through the night, straining our eyes through the darkness, hoping against hope to see the boat coming round the headland.

The dawn came, but there was still no boat, and bitterly disappointed we were forced to the conclusion that it did not mean to return. In addition to our disappointment, we were all very worried, for we felt that another landing from the Japanese was about due. The native soldiers, we noticed, were very nervous and jittery, and we were afraid that they would make a poor showing if we should be attacked. When one of them accidentally fired his rifle, there was a general stampede —we were pretty certain that very few of them would stand up to real fire. After consultation, Jim and I and Bruce, together with another American, Ken Bailey, decided to pay a visit to H.Q. to say that, if we were obliged to remain in the neighbourhood, we needed money, boots, cigarettes, atebrin tablets, and, most urgent of all, a tommy-gun apiece. We felt that if only we were armed with tommy-guns, we could give a good account of ourselves, should the Japanese attack.

But neither our requests, nor we ourselves, were at all well received. All we got was a pair of boots each, some atebrin, and eight packets of cigarettes. Tommy-guns, which we wanted most of all, were not forthcoming. We made our way back from Lingian, sick at heart, and feeling sore and unwanted, and very uneasy as to what might lie ahead.

The next morning we tried to hire a vinta to take us down the coast, for we all wanted to get away from the river mouth, which we thought was a danger spot. But although there were twenty or more vintas drawn up on the beach, none of the owners would take us. At last, finding that politeness did not pay, Jim decided to try tough measures. He decided that we should borrow one and began to push it towards the water. That did the trick all right. Immediately a man sprang up and volunteered to take us wherever we wanted to go.

" I wonder what would have happened if the Japs had wanted a vinta," remarked Bruce as we pushed off.

" I know what would have happened all right," said Ken. " They would have taken it and the skin of the owner for good measure ! "

When we got to the dangerous corner, which we christened Hell's Bend, we all lay flat on the bottom of the boat, just in case the Japs were looking out from their Observation Post across the way. Soon after we had passed this, we saw a quiet little bay where we could land unseen by the enemy, and we made the owner of the vinta pull in to the shore, where we got out. Jim paid the fare, and then, looking around, we came upon two small cottages, both empty and to let. The owner, a Mrs. Barnes, a Philippino, was a widow. Her American husband had died some years previously, and she was now living in her brother's house, together with an eighteen-year-old son. Although we had no money to pay the rent, we were allowed to live in the two cottages, and Jim and I took possession of one, and Bruce and Ken of the other. Jim was suffering from another attack of malaria, so he went straight to bed, and I constituted myself nurse.

When I had got Jim settled with a couple of atebrin, I went to have a chat with Mrs. Barnes. We talked about past raids and possible future ones chiefly. She told me that the last time the Japs had landed on this island, it was right at her front door.

" But I shouldn't think they would come again to same place, should you ? " she said.

I did not feel able to reassure her. It seemed to me that, if they had made a successful landing once, it was just exactly the sort of thing they would do. Ken and I walked with her to the water's edge, and she showed us the spot where the last landing had taken place. It was an ideal landing-place for shallow craft, for they could drift right up to the front door of the house where Mrs. Barnes and her brother lived. Ken, and Bruce, and I, went into conference to discuss the matter. We all felt that it was extremely likely that another landing would take place, and if it did we, with only our revolvers, would be practically useless. Bruce produced his for our inspection. It was about four inches long, and fitted snugly into the palm of his hand. All right for very close range shooting, but no good for any distance. I did not think it would do twenty yards, but Bruce said that it would, and told us to see him blow the bow off a small vinta which was drawn up on the beach.

He took careful aim and pressed the trigger. Apart from a slight click, there was no noise. There was no hole in the vinta, either! Nor anywhere near it. The bullet had dropped practically at Bruce's feet. If he were to hit anyone with that revolver, he would have to throw it at them—and though I was desperately worried about the situation, I couldn't help joining with the others in laughing at this ridiculous state of affairs.

The next day, Ken and Bruce decided to sail on to Baroy, a little farther along the coast, to see if they could contact Colonel Bowler, who, it was rumoured, was due there very shortly, and try to persuade him to give us more suitable arms and some hand grenades. With these, we felt that we could give a good account of ourselves in the event of a Japanese landing. They managed to hire a vinta, and set off, sailing the boat themselves. Jim was better again, and he joined me in a little walk to survey our surroundings, and to map out an escape route in case one should be needed. Not that we were scared of the Japs, but with the weapons we had, we knew that it would be useless to try to oppose them. There was no sense in committing suicide.

At about half past one that same day—it was the twenty-first of January, 1944—we caught sight of three Japanese launches moving southwards along the opposite side of the bay. They appeared to be heading towards Boni-Facio, the village which Jim and I had visited at Christmas. An hour later, we observed another launch, moving in the same direction and towing three barges. These barges could carry about fifty men apiece—a nice compact party for a cut-and-run raid. Also, just the right size to fall into an ambush if we could arrange one. We went at once to the nearest station, and sent a runner off on foot with a message to Colonel Bowler, telling him of our observations, and begging him to send us some arms. But we never got any reply to our message, and to this day I do not know if it was ever received.

All that afternoon we watched people hurrying along the roadway to hide in the jungle, carrying with them as much as they could manage in the way of food and personal belongings. Jim and I wondered if it wouldn't be wise to go with them, but we kept hoping that Bruce and Ken would return, bringing with them the weapons we needed so urgently. In any case, we could not well go off without our two friends, leaving them, perhaps, on their return, to the mercy of the Japanese. About four o'clock, Ken appeared alone. Bruce was still in Baroy, hunting for the Colonel, but up to the time when Ken had left him, he had met with no success. We all sat smoking and talking for another two or three hours, hoping that Bruce would turn up with at least one tommy-gun and a load of grenades. At the place where the Japs had landed before, in front of Mrs. Barnes's home, the jungle came right down to the water, and would afford excellent cover. It would be a simple matter for us to throw the grenades at the landing-party, and then escape into the jungle—if only we had the grenades.

At about eight o'clock, Ken and I began to stroll to the beach to have another look around, leaving Jim in the house. We had only gone a very little way when Mrs. Barnes came rushing up to us and collapsed practically in our arms. The Japs, she told us, breathlessly, were coming in towards the beach. They would land again in front of her house. We could have torn our hair in vexation. Here we were, right in the best possible position to ambush the enemy, and we hadn't a thing to shoot with. If only the Colonel had listened to us and supplied us with suitable arms!

But it was of no use to think of that now. We had to act

quickly. We hurried back to tell Jim what was happening, collected our gear, and then sent Mrs. Barnes and her son, together with Jim, who was still far from well, to wait a little way up the road, while Ken and I went back to the beach to see if the Japanese were really landing. We crept back carefully and stealthily, in the silent way which Joo Meng had taught me, neither of us making a sound or disturbing a twig. Sure enough, the Japanese were making a landing. They were getting out of their barges, talking loudly, and not making any attempt to keep quiet. There was nothing secret about this raid. Helping them to land was a Philippino, holding up a lamp to guide them in. From our position we saw a Japanese officer come forward and shake him by the hand. Full of disgust, Ken and I turned to go back to Jim and the others, when suddenly I thought.

" I might be able to hit him! I'll take a chance!" And drawing my automatic, I took aim and pulled the trigger. To my delight, that Fifth Columnist and his lamp splashed into the water. Another traitor's career was ended!

Creeping back, Ken and I joined Jim and the Barneses, and we made our way to a hide-out in the jungle that Mrs. Barnes had arranged for her and her family's use. There was not much sleep for any of us that night. We were all on the alert, listening intently for any sound that should tell us the enemy was on our track. I longed for a cigarette, but in the circumstances I had to forgo smoking. It might have guided the Japs to our hiding-place. We just sat listening to spasmodic firing from both sides of us, until, towards dawn, it died away.

When daylight came, we crept out to reconnoitre, and finding that the Japanese had gone we returned to our houses. Poor Mrs. Barnes found that her cottage had been looted. When we went down to see how her home had fared, we found her crying bitterly for she had lost practically everything. It was wicked the way the Japanese stole or destroyed civilian possessions everywhere they went.

Five days later, on the twenty-sixth of January, I received a message from the local signal station. It ran : " O.P., 2.30 p.m., 21 Jan. 44., about Ounif farm fulpact on willarms soldiers could be seen in Misamis war ready to ride on mother launch and 2 baby launches. They must be in mission probably in 105 Inf. area. end (sgd) J. Gonia." This cryptic communication, when deciphered, read : " About 150 uniformed and fully-packed, well-armed soldiers can be seen on the Misamis wharf ready to go on board a large launch and two small launches. They will be on a mission, probably in the 105 Infantry area." The station from which it was sent was less than a mile away, yet it took five days for it to reach me! As I have pointed out before, time, and date, and distance, mean nothing at all to these people.

The days passed slowly. Then, early in the afternoon on February the first, Jim and I saw Bruce coming along the road towards us. We were thankful to see him again, for we had worried a good deal as to what had happened to him. It seemed that he had been searching everywhere for Colonel Bowler, but had only succeeded in finding him that very day. He produced cigarettes, and we all three sat down on the grass to smoke and listen to his story. It proved to be a tale of woe. Opening his bag, he displayed a little clothing, a pair of boots, and a few dollars, and a letter which he handed over to me.

" It's from Steele. You'd better read it," he said.

I studied the letter. There was no mention in it of the messenger we had sent, or of our urgent request for weapons. Instead there was a caustic remark, asking if we were lighting our cigarettes with the dollar bills, followed by an order stating that Jim and Bruce were to cross the bay and go back to 105 Divisional headquarters, while I was to go to Lalla. I was very upset and concerned when I read this note. The Japanese were patrolling up and down the bay continually, and to cross it just then would be sheer suicide. Jim and Bruce were upset, too, but when I tried to persuade them not to go, they said that orders were orders and must be obeyed.

" That's all very well," I said. " Orders are orders if they are legitimate orders. But this order really isn't legitimate. It's the biggest bag of bullshit I've ever read."

But they would not listen to my arguments. I walked with

them part of the way, still trying to persuade them not to go, or, if they felt they must, then to cross under cover of darkness. When we parted company, they to try to find a vinta; and I to go to Lalla, I was very angry and unhappy. It seemed such a senseless thing to do—to send two good men to almost certain death when there was surely no real reason for such an order.

On reaching Lalla, I sought out Mr. Soques, and was enjoying a cup of coffee with him, when Jim and Bruce walked in. I almost jumped for joy, hoping that they had changed their minds about making that dangerous crossing and would stay with me. But they still meant to do it, only, after talking it over, they had decided to take my advice and wait at least until after dark. That time came all too quickly, and although Mr. Soques added his pleas to mine, declaring that to cross the bay with Japanese boats now patrolling it all the time was madness, off they went to obey the suicide order.

That very same night, a rush message arrived by runner, saying that all three of us were to return at once to Liangan. If ever I was mad, I was mad then! What were the authorities up to? Had they forgotten that they had sent Bruce and Jim off to almost certain death? I must, of course, try to find them. I called up the local barrio chief and had runners sent out to look for them, though I had very little idea of where by this time they might be. They might already be on the water—how could they be got back then? I wanted to go and search myself, but did not like to leave in case news came while I was gone. All I could do was to stay where I was, and await results. I walked up and down the jungle track outside Mr. Soques's house, miserable and restless and full of foreboding as to what might be happening to my friends. The local C.O. joined me presently and walked up and down with me. All through the night we paced the track, straining our ears to hear sounds of returning searchers. But all we heard were the usual jungle noises, so familiar to me by this time.

Dawn came but brought no news, and I was almost in despair. The morning passed even more slowly than the night had done, and I had practically given up any hope of ever seeing Jim and Bruce again, when sounds outside the house brought me to my feet in a hurry, and there, weary and hungry were the two lost men. They had been found before they could embark on that dangerous voyage, and brought safely back again.

CHAPTER XI

WAITING FOR A SUBMARINE

A F T E R A rest and a cup of coffee, we thanked Mr. and Mrs. Soques for all they had done for us, and started on our journey back to Liangan. We were all three feeling on the top of the world, for we were fairly certain that our recall meant that the big sail boat had returned and we should soon be on our way home. Our optimism was justified. We had to wait a few more days for weather conditions to be favourable, then, at six o'clock on the seventeenth of February, we were told that the boat had entered the river mouth over-night and as soon as she had discharged her cargo we were to embark.

We were wild with excitement. Like little children we hurriedly finished our breakfast and made at top speed for the river and our boat. We stood watching the unloading of the stores she carried, determined this time not to let her out of our sight. While we were watching, a young lieutenant came up and talked to us. He pointed to a clump of trees and told us that it was there that Charlie Wagner had been killed.

" And see that bridge?" he added, indicating a bridge over the river. " We hope to re-name it ' Wagner Bridge '."

We felt that this was a wonderful gesture, and an honour for Australia as well as for the friend whom we had loved.

When the unloading was completed, we decided to take matters into our own hands and not wait for anybody else to tell us to go aboard. We didn't mean to let the boat go off without us this time. So we said goodbye to Rex and Jock, who had come to see us off, and then engaged a vinta to paddle us out to our ship, where we were welcomed by Major Zapanta, the master. During the waiting period, we watched the other passengers embarking, and to our delight we found that one of them was Ray. We had thought that he intended staying in the Philippino Forces, but it seemed that he had changed his mind. We exchanged notes about our various adventures, and we growled a bit to him over the chance we missed when the Japanese landed through not having had the weapons for which we had begged. Ray told us that our messages had never been received, which, in view of the length of time some of Colonel Bowler's orders to us had taken on the way, was quite believable.

About three o'clock that afternoon, our engines started and we moved smoothly out of the river and steered towards the headlong. Look-outs were posted on various parts of the ship to keep a sharp watch for enemy craft. The ship had an all-over length of a hundred feet, with a twelve-foot beam. She drew seven feet of water, and in addition to her engines, had two masts for sails. Of course she was only a small ship, but to us, after the life we had been leading for so long, she seemed very large, and it was hard to believe that we were not dreaming, but were really moving towards the civilisation we knew at last. Hearing the time bells for the change of watches brought the fact home to me, I think, most of all.

There were no bunks to sleep in, so we just stayed where we were through the night. We all slept quite well, though, for when one is thoroughly tired it is possible to sleep in any position, and it was pleasant to wake up with the sea air on our faces as the sun rose above the horizon. The weather was mild and beautifully calm, the sea like a pond, hardly showing a ripple.

Soon after we had breakfasted, we rounded Alubijia Head and entered the bay of Alubijia. On shore we could see the smoke from many fires, and guessed that the Japs must be there, enjoying their usual job as fire-bugs. Five of the soldiers we had aboard had wanted to be landed on the shore of the bay, and the boat put in to allow them to disembark. But the skipper decided to wait a few minutes to make sure that they were all right, and it was as well for them that he did so, for in a very short time they came running back, saying that they could see the Japanese. So we took them aboard again, and went on to another place, Tagababanga Bay, where the lads got off to make their way inland to their homes.

The skipper decided to stay in this bay for a few days, so several of us decided to wade ashore and do a little exploring. Jim and I, of course, went together, paddling through some two hundred yards of shallow water to the beach, which was bordered by coconut trees. Behind the coconuts was a plantation of paw paws, the fruit of which was ripe. An elderly man appeared from somewhere, and sold us a beautiful fruit, about fifteen inches long for four cents—about a penny. We divided it between us, and sitting down on the beach we made a luscious meal from it. Then, lighting up, we sat for a while gazing dreamily into space.

Our peace was broken soon, though, by a Japanese plane which circled over our heads. The crew on board the boat hurried to man the anti-aircraft guns, but the plane scented danger and kept high. It circled three times, then made off in an easterly direction. Those of us who had landed went back to the boat pretty soon after that. There was no sense sitting on the beach watching her sail off without us. Not that we really thought she would, but we felt that it was as well to make sure she didn't.

Later, that afternoon, a submarine chaser steamed into the bay and came up to have a look at us. She kept, though, a good six hundred yards away. Had she come within range of our guns it would have been an easy matter to sink her, for, although she was very swift, her structure was light. But she, too, took good care to keep well away, and after a while she went off.

These two incidents decided Major Zapanta not to make the two-day stay he had intended, and after darkness fell he put to sea again, saying that it wasn't sensible to stay there waiting for trouble.

" The more trouble avoided, the more work one can do," he told us, and we all accepted this as a wise philosophy.

So on we went. Our evenings were very quiet on that boat.

No lights were allowed, for complete darkness was a necessity, so all one could do was to sleep, or sit and look at the stars and smoke. It was not long before trouble came—somehow I never seemed able to avoid it. The engine broke down when we were crossing Cagayan Bay, and it was a case of drifting until repairs were made. They were made pretty quickly and off we went once more. But not for long. A second breakdown occurred, and this time it had us very worried indeed. Our position was between Quinoguitan Point and Camiguan Island, and the Japanese were in residence at both these places.

"What a position to be in!" said Jim, and "It could hardly be worse," I answered.

There was nothing we could do though at present, except sit still and refrain from worrying the crew, who, it was obvious, were already nervous enough. If the worst came to the worst, Ray and I could manage a gun which would be of some value. Meanwhile we must just wait patiently and hope for the best, but fortunately the natives couldn't rush off into the jungle and leave us alone this time. All they could do was to say their prayers and sweat it out with the rest of us.

A slight breeze came along and up went the sails, two big brown beauties. The wind was hardly enough to fill them and we just crawled along. Still, even a crawl was something, it was better than remaining stationary. Even a slow-moving target is more difficult to hit than a sitting one.

At last the engine gave a kick and our hopes rose. Another kick, and then she had started up properly and away we sped. All went merrily now, and soon the major was telling us that the village ahead of us was Butuan, our next destination. Owing, however, to some terrific storms which had lately been experienced, the Agusan River was in heavy flood, and we should have to disembark at a beach some distance away, and be taken on to Butuan by motor lorry.

Very soon we had dropped anchor, and after saying good-bye to Major Zapanta and his crew, Bruce, Ray, Jim and myself were ferried to the beach to await the lorry. It seemed to us incredible that such a vehicle could be available for our transport in enemy-held territory such as this island was. But sure enough, as soon as darkness had fallen, we saw coming towards us, the headlights of a large car. It was the lorry, and I gaped at it in astonishment as it drew up beside us. The more I saw of this war in the Pacific, the more perplexed I became.

We jumped into the truck and began our sixteen-mile journey along a beautiful tarred road. It was strange to be riding in a truck again. It seemed years since we had been in one. The headlights blazed, lighting up the trees and shrubs and houses that bordered the road. It took us Australians back to the days when we were in camp together, before we fell into the hands of the Japs, when we used to ride along laughing and singing, without a care in the world. I felt as though, at last, I had thrown off the shackles of the past years and was really living in freedom again. I looked at the others, and saw that they were just as happy as I was. From the jubilant looks on our faces, no one would have guessed that we were veterans of all the hardships, cruelties, and tortures, we had endured.

At Butuan we were met by Captain Oliver of the U.S.F.I.P In spite of the late hour, he had a big meal waiting for us, with a jug of hot coffee, to send us warm and satisfied to bed. The next morning, the Captain told us that we were to be sent up the river to wait in a safe place until the submarine came to take us back to Australia. We were to leave directly after breakfast, and we would be going by motor launch. Motor launch? Submarine? I wondered if I was really hearing correctly. Only a few days ago, I was dodging Japs in a deadly jungle—now, it seemed, I was back in a civilised world again. I felt quite dazed, everything was happening so fast.

We had our breakfast and then hurried down to the river, to see if there really was a launch there. To our astonishment there were several of them, and all of them flying the Stars and Stripes at the stern. This was, indeed, a sight for sore eyes, and Jim and I nearly fell into the water with the shock of it. When the welcome order came to go on board we lost no time in obeying it, and a few minutes later we were speeding up what seemed to me then to be the most beautiful river in the world. The river was beautiful, the trees were beautiful, the grass was beautiful, everything was beautiful as we sped along in what seemed to us to be an almost unbelievably wonderful dream.

After two delightful hours, our journey came to an end at the riverside village of Amparo. Bruce and Jim and I alighted here, leaving Ray to go on further to the secluded hide-out of Colonel W. W. Fertig, who was acting as commanding general of the Philippino Forces. We three were taken to the home of Lieutcnant and Mrs. Masters, where we were introduced to a party of servicemen, all of whom were waiting for the submarine to take them away for leave. There were now sixteen of us, nine Yanks, one Norwegian, three civilians, and Jim, Bruce, and myself.

Mrs. Masters, a beautiful and attractive Philippino woman, seemed delighted to have us all, and to enjoy all the skylarking that went on. She supervised all the cooking, and though their kitchen was very small she managed wonderfully. The meals were the best I had had for many a long day. The Masters had their own private rice mill just outside the back door, and their own electric light plant. I stared in such astonishment at seeing all the light globes and switches out here in this Never-Never Land, that one of the Yanks thought I was a regular hill-billy of the old-fashioned sort, and he called out:

" Say, fella! All you do is to press this here switch, and see —there is the light! Got it?"

Then began another period of waiting. Our hosts had provided all kinds of games to help us pass the time. There were cards, bingo, dominoes, crib, darts, and many other indoor games. There was a tame monkey, too, which quickly became the pet of us all. The little villain enjoyed himself immensely with such a crowd to play with—there were so many things to pinch, so many pencils to chew up, so many mischievous things all ready for a monkey to do.

Betting as to when the submarine would arrive was one of our chief pastimes. The bets would be laid, and then somebody would take up a position on the veranda to watch for the coming of the launch which would take us down to the mouth of the river. We would know the launch because in it there would be a white-haired old man with a neatly-trimmed snow-white beard—the Colonel himself—and when he appeared we would know that the time had come. Jim and I were among the most eager of the watchers. Hour after hour we would sit with our eyes fixed on the river, and whenever a boat appeared, a shout would bring all the others tumbling out to see if it was the one we were looking for. A prolonged groan of " No-o-o !" would proclaim their disgust when they found that it wasn't, and back they would go to their cards and their cribbage again.

On the twenty-second of February, we experienced a real tropical storm. The rain poured down in torrents, and the river began to rise. Higher and higher it rose, until the water was up to floor level. The rice mill was flooded and the electric light plant was thrown out of action. But neither of these catastrophes worried Mrs. Masters. She just pulled out her canoe, and with the skill of a professional she paddled it across the flooded river to the other side, picked up the stores she needed, and returned as calmly and coolly as if she had only had to walk out to the back shed. This ferrying business had to be carried on for several days as, even after the rain had stopped, the water still came rushing down, bringing with it logs and trees and other debris. On two occasions, whole houses drifted by.

From time to time launches would come up from the mouth of the river, bringing goods or mail, tying up to the veranda while the owners delivered their cargoes. Each new arrival was greeted by us with a rousing cheer, which usually caused the boatman to stare at us as if we were screwy and then go quickly away. This waiting and watching business, which we kept up day and night, working in relays, was trying for some of the others but for Jim and me it was nothing. We had done so much of it in the past in such dangerous and uncomfortable circumstances, that just to sit back in easy chairs, smoking, was a pleasant holiday.

The morning of the twenty-ninth of February dawned. It was a beautiful morning, the sun was shining, the birds were singing, the butterflies were dancing over our heads. Then suddenly, cruising down the river, came an unusually large launch. We all rushed to the railings to watch it approach, and a great cheer went up when we saw a man with a white beard in it. The craft for which we had been waiting and watching had come at last. We did not need to be told to pack. Our things had been packed and waiting for days, and when Lieutenant Masters came and told us that we were to start the next morning and we had better get ready, there was really nothing for us to do.

I think that day was about the longest I ever remember. The hours simply dragged past. Nobody could settle down to playing games. Cards were left untouched, nobody so much as opened a book. When the monkey climbed up to the ceiling with one of our caps, nobody bothered to throw a crust at him to bring him down. We just walked backwards and for-wards from the house to the veranda, stopping every few minutes to have a look at the clock to see how far the hands had moved. It was a relief to everybody when dark came and one by one we fell asleep.

Before dawn we were all awake again. It was the first of March, my birthday, and while we were eating our breakfast Jim suddenly remembered it, and turned to me said : " Happy birthday, Wal !" That sent the whole crowd of them on to their feet, singing *Happy Birthday*, and I received so many and such hearty slaps on the back, that my breath was quite taken away. Before the excitement of this interlude had sub-sided, a large launch tied up outside and the skipper shouted out :

" All bags first, please !"

A wild scramble then took place. Nobody finished breakfast. Bags were gathered and slung on board, and after we had thanked all the folk who had been so kind and generous to us, we followed our luggage on to the launch and the down-river journey began.

The excitement had made my heart jump about in a most peculiar way. I could feel it throbbing violently, and I kept getting giddy turns. I wondered what could be the matter, and I felt so queer that I saw little of the country during our

L

voyage down the river. It was not until the boat came to a stop at the river-mouth that I came to life again and began to look about me. When I did, I saw that many other launches were moving around, all flying the Stars and Stripes, and all, apparently, having important business to perform. So much activity was going on, so openly and unconcernedly, that a casual observer would have found it hard to believe that a powerful enemy was present in force at only a few miles' distance.

Not far from where our launch was anchored, a square-shaped barge was floating, hidden under the trees that over-hung the river-bank. It was decorated with shrubs and palms and other greenery, so that, viewed from a little way off, it looked exactly like a tiny island. This barge was, we learned, to be towed out to the submarine when it came, and used to bring back stores and army comforts which the submarine would be bringing for the Underground Fighters. Should any enemy planes or gunboats appear the barge would stay motion-less until they had gone. Her camouflage was so perfect that they would be unlikely to guess that she was anything other than one of the small islets with which the coastal waters here were dotted.

Apart from eating the meals which had been arranged for us, all we had to do was to sit around and wait until the submarine should come, when the launch would take us out to it. The news that it was expected had spread, and many of the local inhabitants had gathered to see its arrival and to wish us god-speed when we embarked in it. The centre of all activity was the Colonel's radio, which was set up close by, with the Colonel waiting to get in touch with the sub-marine as soon as it was reported in the vicinity. Few of us took our eyes from him, as we waited and waited through the long hours. The sun sank down, darkness fell, yet still the sub-marine did not come, and at last we were told that we must return to Butuan for the night.

It was midnight when a down-hearted bunch of servicemen reached Butuan. We were given a cup of coffee, then we dossed down where we could to sleep. We did sleep, too, in spite of the discomfort, for we were all so tired. The next day, after an anxious morning, the launch came to pick us up about two o'clock in the afternoon, and once more we headed for the mouth of the river. When we got there, we found that the people had gathered in hundreds, waiting for the big moment when the submarine should be reported. More waiting ensued, then, just after sunset, a rumour spread that Colonel Fertig was in touch by radio with the submarine.

Excitement rose to fever pitch, and Bruce and I, who with many of the others of our party had gone ashore, raced down to the beach, hoping to get a glimpse of the submarine through the gathering darkness. We strained our eyes but there was nothing to be seen—only a darkening expanse of greyness, with the line of white surf where the waves broke on the beach.

All at once we sighted something—a long, grey shape, darker than the greyness around it. Yes, it was the submarine. My heart missed a beat, and though I tried to speak, I could not. Words just would not come. I looked at Bruce and saw that he was in the same boat. But speech was not really needed. We both knew what to do. With one accord, we took to our heels and raced back to tell the others what we had seen.

Never in my life had I seen men go so wild with enthusiasm as we all did then. Hats were thrown into the air, we kissed and hugged each other, we shouted and cheered, and cheered and shouted, until no one had any breath left to shout and cheer longer. Then, as the first uproar died down, we heard the voice of our skipper.

"All aboard!" he shouted, and in a matter of seconds we were all in the launch, heading out in the darkness towards the submarine. There was a huge swell on, and the launch rocked and tossed as she left the shelter of the river-mouth, and spray splashed over us repeatedly. But none of us worried about that. The submarine for which we had waited, of which we had talked and dreamed for so long, was there. We could all see her now, looming up in the darkness, the most wonderful sight in the world, a long, slender, grey object, with a huge conning tower in the centre and what appeared to be a six-inch gun at either end. Our launch glided along-side it, the submarine's crew put out helping hands, and we were pulled up on to the deck of the United States' Submarine *Narwhal*.

CHAPTER XII

HOMEWARD BOUND

I T W A S a marvellous feeling, finding myself on the deck
of the submarine. It seemed as if a terrific load had suddenly
been lifted from my shoulders, and it was all I could do to
stop myself from crying in my joy. We were quickly ushered
down a spiral stairway and directed as to where we were to
go.

The submarine had to get away as soon as possible so the
stores it had brought were quickly unloaded, and the hatches
closed. Instructions came to us over the public address system,
telling us to sit still where we were. We were moving, but no
movement could be felt, and silence reigned supreme. Then
a klaxon sounded, which, as we learnt later, meant that we
were going to take a " trim dive "—something to do with
adjustment of balance, due to the fact that certain loads were
removed and others taken on.

After a few minutes below, the klaxon again sounded, twice
this time, and we surfaced. We were then told to report to the
mess room for dinner. When we got there we found bread,
butter, and jam, on the table, loads of it, as much as we
wanted. We were given tomato soup, and then a grill. As the
soup was put before me, by feelings got too much for me.
Real tears came into my eyes and I felt frightened to touch it.

" It's good chow. Get stuck into it," said a petty officer,
and plucking up courage I tasted it. The flavour was something
never to be forgotten, and so was that of the grill which
followed. We had been having good food for the last few
weeks, but nothing like this. This was real food, home food—

165

and that first meal on the *Narwhal* is one that I shall never forget.

We returned to the quarters that had been allotted to us, feeling happy and contented, when our happiness was made perfect by the captain's issuing to each of us a carton of Camel cigarettes. Words cannot describe my feelings that night, as Jim and I sat together after that wonderful meal, smoking those cigarettes.

Our movements on board the submarine were very restricted. We were passengers on an armed war vessel, and we had to be careful not to hinder the crew in their duties. The quarters allotted to Jim and me were, however, quite comfortable. They were close to the torpedo room, and from where we sat we could see right into it. One of the petty officers who saw me gazing at the torpedo tubes said to me :

" Only four of them left now. Say, our boys had a great time sinking Jap ships. We got dozens of them a bit down south from here. We sure have a live agent in that neighbourhood."

Then he asked us where we came from, and what we were doing up at the place where we were taken aboard. This was rather a difficult question to answer, for we knew that we had to be discreet in the information we gave away. So I just said that we had been doing a little observation, and that was the reply I made to everyone who asked the same question. We heard a lot from the members of the crew about the many ships they had torpedoed or had sunk by gun fire. They liked the gunfire best, because they saw the target and could see it go down, whereas, with the torpedoes, they were just sent on their way and all the crew heard was the resulting explosion. They all gave great praise to the agent " Down South," who sent them such accurate reports about enemy shipping, but they never knew who the man was who had organised that " agent."

There were piles of magazines and papers available for those who wanted to read, and quite a lot of the crew's time seemed to be spent reading them, or in writing letters home. Our party passed the time mainly in the same occupations. We couldn't move about much, as I have said, because of the

confined space. Toilets and showers were provided at both ends
of the vessel, but if we were submerged, toilets might not be
used, except with express permission. The reason being that
toilet paper would float to the surface and might give away
our position to the enemy.

As a special concession, I was allowed to visit the engine
room. In it were clocks of all shapes and sizes, switches, levers,
and hundreds of wheels. It was a real Chinese puzzle to the
newcomer. I found it very interesting and I paid a visit to it
at least once each day, partly to talk to some new friends
I had found there, but mainly to check our position, and try
to calculate how long it would be before we hit Australia.

For a while most of our travel was on the surface, but towards dusk on the second day, somewhere between the islands
of Negros and Zamboango, the siren sounded, and down we
went. For a moment or two Jim and I did not know if it was
just a practice dive or the real thing. Then the look on the
faces of the men, as they stood alert, waiting for the command which would send them to their stations, told us what
to expect. A target had been sighted, the periscope went up,
then a voice over the system called out :

" Action Stations ! " and like arrows shot from a bow the
men rushed to their various positions and waited to receive
the next order.

Jim and I sat huddled in our corner, watching keenly all
that was happening. The torpedo tubes had been loaded, and
now the silence was awe-inspiring. Then again the voice came,
describing the target. A seven-thousand-ton transport had
been sighted, and the submarine was skilfully and silently
moving in on its prey. The varying ranges were called out,
as the submarine manœuvred about, selecting the most suitable position. The tension became acute to the minutes dragged
by. Then the order came : " Fire No. 1. Fire No. 2. Fire
No. 3. Fire No. 4."

We listened carefully. There were four distinct " swishes "
as the four torpedoes left the tubes on their errands of destruction. Once more there was that deathly silence. Then, all
of a sudden, came a terrific explosion, followed by the voice
of the commander saying :

"We got it, boys! We blew the bow right off the bastard!"

An officer watched through the periscope to see if the target sank, but the watch was not maintained, because the transport's escort, a big Japanese destroyer, was on the warpath, searching for the submarine which had hit her charge. We dived deep down, silence was ordered, and the engines were cut off. We were told not to move or talk, but the lights were left on.

The destroyer was hot on the warpath. It circled round and round above us, and after what seemed an eternity, a sharp metallic ping was heard on our hull.

"They've got on to us," whispered a sailor.

Another agonising wait—then we heard a prolonged swish, followed by an explosion, just above us. We rocked and rolled, the water round us seemed to have become a whirlpool. Then came another swish, another great "boom."

"Depth charges," whispered the sailor.

Round and round went the destroyer, working to a set pattern, dropping charge after charge. Paint flaked off the walls and showered about us, as the submarine rocked more and more violently with each explosion. Twelve depth charges were dropped—then, to our immense relief, there came silence.

It had been a terrifying experience. I felt sick and shaken. Jim, and several members of the crew, actually were sick. I for one, shall never forget my feelings during that bombing. It made an impression on me that will last for all time.

We were down for about two hours. Then the sound of two blasts on the klaxon told us that the danger was over. Those klaxon blasts were sweeter than music to our ears. One could sense the relief that swept over everyone at the sound of them. We surfaced rapidly. The inrush of fresh air nearly deafened those of us who were not used to it. After the stillness and silence below water, the noise above came almost as a shock. But it was wonderful to breath in the freshness and to be able to move about and talk again.

The *Narwhal* was now heading fast for Tawi Tawi. I nearly collapsed when I was told that. Had we passed through all those dangers and hardships only to come right back to the place we had started from?

" Well! Wouldn't that slay you!" I said to Jim.

Late at night on the fifth of March, we stopped off the northern coast of Tawi Tawi. The hatches were swung open and stores for the island were handed out. Soldiers from the depot came out in vintas to bring the precious cargo to shore. I went up on deck to get some fresh air, and to see if I knew any of the men. I was recognised by several of them, and greeted enthusiastically. One of them gave me news of Sandakan, but it was not good news. Many of my comrades, he said, had died in the prison camp, and Heng Joo Meng had been arrested for helping me and others of the Australians. The fingers of his right hand had been cut off as a punishment. But he went on doing the same things and was arrested again, and this time he was executed.

This was a dreadful shock to me. As I stood there, I saw again his smiling face, and thought of his untiring work for me and the other prisoners, his loyalty and devotion, and my heart was full of grief—not only for him, but for the wife in Singapore of whom he had told me, his daughter, Mary, and his son, John. The plans we had made for meeting again after the war was over, would never come true now. Nor was the death of Joo Meng the only bad news the soldier told me. My mate, Frank Martin, was in gaol, so was Sergeant McAlister Blain. Captain Mathews had been executed, and Dr. J. P. Taylor had been beaten up for helping me and for supplying drugs to the camp, and sentenced to fifteen years penal servitude. Many others who had helped us had also been executed.

I was so near to tears that I moved away from my informant and went towards the nearest hatch, for I felt that I must get below where I could be alone to think over all this dreadful news. It was lucky for me that I did so, for suddenly, without any warning the hatches were slammed down and locked. I just had time to slip inside the one I was standing by before it was closed. The moment they were shut, the submarine dived below and slipped away into deep water. Later, we learned that the radar screen had shown two warships approaching, one from each end of the island. Evidently fifth columnists were still active in Tawi Tawi and had informed the enemy of the submarine's visit.

The *Narwhal* had submerged so unexpectedly and so quickly, that those who were on the top and couldn't reach the hatchway in time were washed overboard, while those who were trapped down below had to come on with us to Darwin. Among the company we had picked up, I found Captain Hamner and Lieutenant Kane, who had joined us with two Australians and one Englishman. The two Americans, Hamner and Kane, were well. We had much to say to one another, and among other things I was told that the Tawi Tawi Signal Corps had been responsible for the sinking of approximately sixty Japanese ships in the waters round the island. This news almost overwhelmed me. I knew that the men I had trained had been the cause of some sinkings, but I had never dreamed that the score was so great. I felt on top of the world! It was marvellous to know that the work I had started had brought about such colossal results.

I did not say much at the time, but later, with the help of some of the submarine's staff, we worked out figures which showed that through my Signal Station Japan had lost roughly 130,000 tons of shipping, and about 150,000 soldiers. It was a wonderful result, and my heart was full of gratitude to the men who had carried out my instructions so faithfully, and to Joo Meng, the man who had made my escape from Sandakan possible, so enabling me to organise the corps which had brought about those sinkings.

That narrow escape off Tawi Tawi was the last of my really dangerous adventures. For the rest of the voyage, we were on the surface for most of the time. We had one more alarm, when the klaxon sounded and we dived below, but it was only a plane which the radar screen had picked up, and as soon as it had gone we surfaced again. The trip became rather boring, for we had nothing to do but eat and sleep, play cards and read, and pay visits to the engine room. After the life we had been leading, this existence seemed monotonous in the extreme.

Then one day, a bulletin was posted up on the notice board saying that we were due in Darwin on March the eleventh —just two more days. Those last two days seemed as if they would never pass, but they went at last, and on the eleventh of March, 1944, the submarine dropped anchor a few miles out of Darwin. A patrol boat came out to take us off, we said goodbye to our hosts of the *Narwhal*, and a few minutes later we were heading fast for the shore.

There is not much more to tell. I was so overcome with emotion when I found myself standing once more on Australian soil, that I knelt down and kissed the ground, much to the amusement of those who were around. We spent the first night in army tents, in the quarantine section, to which we had been taken as soon as we landed for inspection and overhaul. We lay on army stretchers, still with our boots on, and brushed away the millions of flies that attacked us—just like old times Jim and I said, as we surveyed the bare, cracked floorboards and drab surroundings, which had been so familiar to us in our training days. One event, though, was not like those days. A lad suddenly appeared before us, holding a tray on which were standing two clean glasses and two bottles of iced beer.

" For you, sir," he said.

The next day we were flown to Brisbane, where we were met by Brigadier J. D. Roberts of the Australian Intelligence Section, who took us in a staff car to his headquarters where they told me that I was the first Australian prisoner of war to escape successfully from a Japanese prison camp, and the *only* one to escape from Sandakan and arrive in Australia. Our families, they said—Jim's, Ray's, and mine—had been notified of our arrival, but we had to stay in Brisbane for a few days to give us much information to the Intelligence Section as we could. I was able to hand over the letter enrusted to me by McAlister Blain, which was a great relief to me. Through all my adventures I had managed to bring it safely back.

While at Brisbane, I was put on the scales and weighed. From fourteen stone, seven pounds, I had dropped to seven stone—no wonder I had been able to get under the barbed wire! While we were there, too, the late Field Marshal Sir Thomas Blamey called and congratulated us on what we had done. " Most astounding," was his remark upon our achievement.

From Brisbane, we were flown to Sydney—for me, home.

My malaria came on in the plane, but, ill as I was, I forced myself up to look out of the window as we approached the town, feasting my eyes once more upon those glorious sights —the rugged coast line, the harbour, the bridge. Lieutenant-Colonel Prentice was at Rose Bay to meet us, and seeing the condition that I was in—by this time I was really frightfully ill—he packed me quickly into his staff car and rushed me to the Concord Repatriation Hospital, while Jim was driven to the Sydney Show Ground to await transport to Melbourne.

It was on the twenty-fourth of March, eleven months after my escape, that Sister quietly opened the door of the private ward where I had been placed for security reasons, and ushered in, for a few brief moments, my daughter and my wife. It was then, as we all three embraced each other, that I realised I was at last back home.

POSTSCRIPT

AFTER I had recovered from the malaria, and from an operation for double hernia, I was sent to Melbourne for further interrogation by the Intelligence Section. I was anxious to go back to Sandakan to help in the rescue of my mates, but though I did all in my power to induce the authorities to send a raiding-party to the island, my efforts met with no success. I learnt later that they were afraid to make any attempt at rescue for fear that the Japanese should take reprisals in other P.O.W. camps.

Whether they would have done so or not, I cannot say. They were quite capable of it, as I knew to my cost. But, in any case, rescue would probably have come too late to help my friends. The story of Sandakan is a terrible one. After my escape, about a hundred of the officers were moved to Kuching. Most of these lived to return home. The rest of the Sandakan prisoners were marched from Sandakan to the Ranau Valley, a distance of about a hundred and sixty-five miles, over jungle terrain that would have been appallingly difficult even for fit men. For our poor fellows, sick, broken, and half-starved, it was a death march. Only six of them survived the ordeal. Of the original fifteen hundred prisoners of Sandakan, only those six, together with the hundred Kuching officers and a handful of men who had been gaoled for various reasons and so escaped the march, came home. Frank, I am thankful to say, was one of the gaoled men. I met him when he arrived in Sydney. It was a wonderful reunion.

Dr. Taylor, the courageous medical officer who had smuggled drugs into the camp, had, as I had heard, been arrested and tortured, and sentenced to fifteen years' penal servitude. Later, he was condemned to death, but the bomb on Japan came in time to save his life, and I am glad to say he returned to Australia becoming Medical Superintendent of the Concord Repatriation General Hospital of New South Wales.

Lieutenant Hosijimah met with his just deserts. After the war he was arrested, tried, found guilty of major atrocities, and executed as a war criminal, a fate he most richly deserved.

As for me, I have had much appreciation and kindness shown to me for the job that I did. The experiences through which I passed have taken their inevitable toll of my health, but despite that I look back with pride and some measure of content at what we were able to accomplish in squaring accounts with a vicious enemy.

PUBLISHER'S NOTE

For his escape, and for his work in the Philippines, the Author was Mentioned in Dispatches for " Distinguished Service in the South-West Pacific Area " (*Commonwealth of Australia Gazette*, 34/46). This was followed by the award of the Bronze Star Medal from the President of the United States. (*Commonwealth of Australia Gazette*, 122/48), which reads :

The King has been graciously pleased to grant unrestricted permission for the wearing of the following decoration, which has been conferred upon the undermentioned in recognition of services rendered in the cause of the Allies.
AUSTRALIAN MILITARY FORCES
Conferred by the President of the United States of America:
" The Bronze Star Medal "—*Warrant Officer Walter Wallace, NX* 58809.

The Citation for the Bronze Star Medal

Warrant Officer Walter Wallace, NX 58809, A.I.F. Performed meritorious service at Tawi Tawi, Sulu, Philippines, from July to October, 1943. As Regimental Signal Officer, he demonstrated efficiency in the operation of the signal unit 125th Infantry Regiment (Guerillas). His submission of timely information regarding the presence of enemy shipping in the Sulu and Celebes Seas resulted in their destruction. His judicious decision and devotion to duty was a source of inspiration to the men in his unit and reflected the highest credit on the service.